CHORUSES

CHORUSES

Poems by Quincy Troupe

COFFEE HOUSE PRESS

Some of these poems first appeared in the following magazines: ZYZZYVA, *A Gathering of the Tribes*, *Tin House*, *Review: Latin American Literature and Arts*, *Downtown Review*, *Code*, *Indiana Review*, *Brilliant Corners*, and *Long Shot*.

Coffee House Press is an independent nonprofit literary publisher supported in part by a grant provided by the Minnesota State Arts Board, through an appropriation by the Minnesota State Legislature, and in part by a grant from the National Endowment for the Arts. Significant support has also been provided by the McKnight Foundation; the Star Tribune Foundation; the Lila Wallace-Reader's Digest Fund; the Bush Foundation; Target Stores, Dayton's, and Mervyn's by the Dayton Hudson Foundation; General Mills Foundation; St. Paul Companies; Butler Family Foundation; Honeywell Foundation; James R. Thorpe Foundation; Pentair, Inc.; the law firm of Schwegman, Lundberg, Woessner & Kluth, P.A.; and many individual donors. To you and our many readers across the country, we send our thanks for your continuing support.

Coffee House Press books are available to the trade through our primary distributor, Consortium Book Sales & Distribution, 1045 Westgate Drive, Saint Paul, MN 55114. For personal orders, catalogs, or other information, write to: Coffee House Press, 27 North Fourth Street, Suite 400, Minneapolis, MN 55401. Good books are brewing at www.coffeehousepress.org.

LIBRARY OF CONGRESS CIP INFORMATION
Troupe, Quincy.
    Choruses : poems / by Quincy Troupe.
       p.   cm.
    ISBN 1-56889-090-X (alk. paper)
    1. Afro-Americans Poetry. I. Title.
    PS3570.R63C48   1999
    881'.54—dc21   99-35487
                                                         CIP

10 9 8 7 6 5 4 3 2 1
first printing/first edition

For my youngest son, Porter Sylvanus Troupe;
to the memory and work of Allen Ginsberg;
and, as always, for my wonderful wife, Margaret,
who is the personification of great living music and spirituality.

CONTENTS

AUTHOR'S NOTE

In January 1996, artist and sculptor Mathieu Gregoire of San Diego asked me to participate as a poet in a collaborative project for The Point Loma Wastewater Treatment Plant in San Diego, California. This unique, innovative project, planned and conceived by Gregoire, brought together engineers, architects, painters, a composer and musician, and landscape architects to help organize a comprehensive plan for the development of the wastewater facility. The project, called "The Report on Landscape, Architectural and Aesthetic Improvements to the Point Loma Wastewater Treatment Plant" is ongoing, and is scheduled for completion around 2004. "The Point Loma Poems" are my contribution to this project. Some of the poems were written for inscriptions to be sandblasted in granite throughout the twenty-five acre facility. Some of them will be outside, inscribed into walls, along paths that look out at the Pacific Ocean. For the most part these are the longer poems. The shorter poems—mostly tankas and haikus—will be inscribed underground on walls where workers work, some-times totally away from sunlight and air. Since the completion of this project is some years in the future I decided to publish versions of the poems in *Choruses*. A more sanitized rendition will be on display when the Point Loma Project is completed.

"The Broken in Parts" poem was written for a theatrical project of the same name, conceived and put together by the great reed player, Oliver Lake. This pro-ject, produced by Unity Concerts of New Jersey, was a year-long collaboration of musicians, actors, dancers, a director, and poets (including me, who conducted poetry workshops for community people), and was centered around the town of Montclair, New Jersey, where Lake lives. The final project was realized as a the-ater production, in which I participated by reading my poem. The piece played to capacity-filled audiences on December 5 – 6, 1998, in Upper Montclair, New Jersey.

I

SONG

words & sounds that build bridges toward a new tongue
within the vortex of cadences, magic weaves there
a mystery, syncopating music rising from breath of the young,

the syllables spraying forward like some cloud or mist hung
around the day, evening, under streetlamps, yeasting air, where
words & sounds that build bridges toward a new tongue

gather, lace the language like fireflies stitching the night's lungs,
rhythms of new speech reinventing themselves with a flair,
a mystery, syncopating music, rising from breath of the young,

where the need for invention at the tongue's edge, high-strung,
at the edge of the cliff, becomes a risk-taking poet who shares
words & sounds that build bridges toward a new tongue,

full of wind & sun, breath feeds poetry from art's aqualungs,
under a blue sea that is sky, language threads itself through air
a mystery, syncopating music, rising from breath of the young,

is a solo snatched from the throat of pure utterance, sung,
or wordsmiths blues-ing cadences, weaving lines into prayers,
words & sounds that build bridges toward a new tongue—
a mystery, syncopating music, rising from breath of the young

SESTINA FOR 39 SILENT ANGELS

there was no screaming to announce hale-bopp comet's second tail,
no screaming when those 39 people left their bodies—
their containers—behind, covered their faces with purple
silk shrouds, folded triangles, lay down smiling & fell into the steep sleep
marshall applewhite had prescribed for them deep inside that death
mansion in rancho santa fe, they knew themselves as angels,

sleuths at creating web sites, cruising the internet, space angels
flying on wings of ancient dreams upward to hale-bopp comet's tail,
(& the only way to get there through the invisible doorway of death)
launched through skies of their minds, they willed their bodies
on earth, as people of jonestown did, to be recycled through sleep,
bodies board-stiff & bloated, looking for peace, skin purple,

going black as the clothes they wore, covered 39 faces with purple
symbols the color of lenten holy week when jesus rose up to join angels,
39 travelers wore black nike shoes, weaved through 39 catacombs of sleep,
dreamed themselves up like 39 shooting stars to hale-bopp comet's tail
of silver ice, where they would transform their bodies—
18 buzz-haired castrated males, 21 females surfing death's

internet—to pass through heaven's-gate's needle eye—& death
not even a stopover here for these souls to rest dressed in black & purple,
quarters for phone calls, 5 dollar bills for whatever urges their bodies
needed—before flying through space 39 dreams, they would be truly angels
rendezvousing with the mothership hidden inside hale-bopp comet's tail,
live with extraterrestrials there in a sleeve of silver ice after sleep

cut them loose to flow through steep mystery above as sleep
like rocket fuel fell away over stages, left them asphyxiated in death
after phenobarbital, apple sauce, & vodka, they knew the silver ice tail
as the sign they were waiting for to cover themselves with shrouds of purple,
leave behind computer screens—skies—they flew purely as angels
now toward a higher source than conflicting urges of their bodies—

a tangle of web sites, conquered & controlled, their bodies—
surrendering the improvisation of living, they swam in sleep,
drifting slowly as motorless boats on the sea—were homeless angels,
took 39 pot pies & cheese cakes for their journey, they kissed death
hard with dry mouths, 39 people down from 1000, pursed lips of purple
open in wonder, they flew up to enter hale-bopp comet's tail

of silver ice particles, gaseous bodies grinning there like death
skulls flashing inside sleep, inside where eye am dreaming now of purple,
faith flashing bright as new angels inside hale-bopp comet's third tail

FORTY-ONE SECONDS ON A SUNDAY IN JUNE, IN SALT LAKE CITY, UTAH

for Michael Jordan

rising up in time, michael jordan hangs like an icon, suspended in space,
cocks his right arm, fires a jump shot for two, the title game on the line,
his eyes two radar screens screwed like nails into the mask of his face

bore in on the basket, gaze focused, a thing of beauty, no shadow, or trace,
no hint of fear, in this, his showplace, his ultimate place to shine,
rising up in time michael jordan hangs like an icon, suspended in space,

after he has moved from baseline to baseline, sideline to sideline, his coal-face
shining, wagging his tongue, he dribbles through chaos, snaking serpentine,
his eyes two radar screens screwed like nails into the mask of his face,

he bolts a flash up the court, takes off, floats in for two more in this race
for glory, it is his time, what he was put on earth for, he can see the headline,
rising up in time, michael jordan hangs like an icon, suspended in space,

inside his imagination, he feels the moment he will embrace, knows his place
is written here, inside this quickening pace of nerves, he will define,
his eyes two radar screens screwed like nails into the mask of his face,

inside this moment he will rule on his own terms, quick as a cat he interfaces
time, victory & glory, as he crosses over his dribble he is king of this shrine,
rising up in time, michael jordan hangs like an icon, suspended in space,
his eyes two radar screens screwed like nails into the mask of his face

SWINGING FOR GLORY

for Mark McGuire & Sammy Sosa

mark mcguire & sammy sosa went into baseball's final weekend
during 1998, like twins, after hitting boatloads of home runs all season,
they were tied two games from the finish, with one last dance & chance
to swing their pulverizing bats for glory at aspirin-sized, marked baseballs
high-tailing it in from the mound straight as taut clotheslines, or hooking back
over corners of plates like snakes trying to escape killer bats,

it was glorious watching them cock, before swinging those clubbing bats,
during this summer of numbing terror & scandal, media-pushed smut, to no end,
all day, each was glorious, took our minds off terror that mccarthy was back,
this time snooping through people's private sex lives, during a terrible season,
when uptight white men & women moved around chopping off balls
of enemies, wielding their razor-sharp media axes, their tongues, by chance

wagging in their puffed-up, polished faces, everything hanging on chance,
evaporating words, hoping to be believable as mark & sammy's mighty bats,
fans all over the world exploding whenever their driving clubs cracked balls,
sent them screaming & skying over distant walls, during the final weekend
hurricane georges approached swinging fury over the gulf, perhaps to season
up that final day, shaped itself, like a ragged baseball, it hooked back,

away from new orleans, in the midnight hour, while sammy tried to fire back,
after mark clotheslined his 70th, sosa stuck on 66, though time left one chance
for him to shine the next day sammy knew it was over, but it had been a season
where both covered themselves in glory, black & white, swinging their bats
in harmony, we watched them unite over a last stormy weekend,
watched two men cheering each other on over the flight of a baseball,

beautiful in their respect for the game, for each other, over hitting a baseball
off radar & richter screens, they stood, white & black, stood back to back,
as a nation pondered oral sex, a president, & a hurricane, during a final weekend
when ultimate glory would come down to a few swings of honed skill & chance,
while statuettes of each player standing in bric-a-bracs swinging their bats
was already a sign each had covered themselves with glory this season,

but it was the beauty & glory of the electric chase throughout the season,
the random coupling of different eyes & hearts watching a screaming baseball
fly over a wall, or clean out of a park, like a frightened bird at the crack of a bat,
it was a chase of two men, neither perfect, in each other's corner, back to back,
after all is said & done, one black, one white, in a country divided by chance,
birth, most found themselves cheering both, over a final, stormy weekend,

it was beautiful, for one baseball season, two men linked themselves back,
with honor to babe ruth & roger maris's towering home run balls, with a chance
both would stand together, as one, over one last, glorious, stormy weekend

FACES

leaves dance tree branches,
shook by wind tongue, glows there, look—
faces in green light

leaves dance tree branches,
shook by wind tongue, faces glow
there, pulse through green light

leaves dance on blue air,
pushed by tonguing breezes, look,
faces break green light

helter-skelter, leaves
dance like faces bobbing in crowds
shake & bake on breezes

leaves dancing in trees,
pushed by tongues of breezes, look
faces in blue light

high in branches, above ground

CAN YOU CHAIN YOUR VOICE TO A RIVER?

woke up one morning, found myself stepping through a dream,
say eye woke up one morning, found myself singing in a dream,
eye was on a road long & narrow, the wind was imitating a scream,
the road eye was on was long & narrow, the wind a substitute for a scream,
so eye kept right on walking, hoping the scream would end,
say eye kept right on stepping, hoping that dream would surely end

in the middle of that dream found myself by a long snaking river,
say in the middle of that screaming dream found myself by a long snaking river,
say that river was sky-deep, moonrays dancing off its back like slivers of silver,
that's when eye ask myself a question, a cool wind making me shiver like liver.
say eye ask myself a question, cool wind making me quiver & shiver like liver

said, "can you chain your voice to a river, swim it to wherever it ends?"
said, "can you chain your voice to a river, swim it to wherever it ends?"
rivers carry their own rhythm, carry their own deadly sins,
say rivers are their own rhythm, are their own deadly sins,
blue skies & storm clouds be hats eye wear, wear till the bitter end,
say blue skies & black clouds be hats eye wear, wear till the wailing end

then eye was walking land by the river, caught up in a surrealist dream,
say eye was walking land beside that river, inside a surrealist dream,
when all of a sudden a cloud hung down, spoke to me in the voice of a poet,
say a dark funnel cloud hung down, spoke to me in the language of a poet,
at first eye heard the voice of Moses, then eye heard God up in that wind,
say first eye thought it was Moses, then eye heard God up in that wind

"go downriver," the Voice in the wind said, "go down it to the very end,
eye say take a boat & go downriver, sail it long to the very end,
listen to a broken man singing from a treetop, listen to his ancient sins,
say listen to a poor man moaning on a tree branch, singing about ancient sins,
that old man was once a great singer, ain't heard him since way back when,
that man used to be a great poet, ain't seen him since way back when

now he weak as a puff of smoke, caught up in a tornado's wind,
say he weak as a wisp of smoke, caught in a tornado's wind,
long ago he was handsome & proud, voice stronger than most men eye knew,
say he was handsome, proud long ago, voice better than most men eye knew,
then hard times came on him like he a vampire caught out in daylight-wind,
say bad times caught him like he a vampire locked outside in sunlight, wind
so he ran away, went underground, found himself in that old gnarled tree
say he ran away, went underground, found himself stuck in a gnarled old tree,
now he need to be talked down out those leafless branches, so he can sing again
say he need to be talked down out those skeletal branches, so he can sing again
need someone show him the light, convince him there's a better road,
say he need someone to be his friend, show him there's a much better road,
it's you my friend can show him that light, help him drop his heavy load,
say it's you my friend can show him light, help him drop his heavy load

so go downriver & find him my son, tell him he can swim & sing again
say go downriver, find him my son, tell him we need him to swim & sing, again
but the only reward eye can promise you will be a song you hear up in the wind,
say the only thing eye can give you will be a song you'ill hear up in the wind,
a song you keep locked in your heart, make you feel good whenever you hear it,
a song you keep locked in your heart, make you feel good each time you hear it,
so go on downriver, find that man, listen for the song up in the wind,
say go on downriver, find that man, listen for that song up in the wind,
when you find him my son you'ill hear yourself singing a sweeter song,
say when you find him my son you'ill find yourself singing a more lyrical song"

after getting over shock of hearing that voice eye get in a canoe, go downriver,
say after getting over shock, hearing that voice eye get in a canoe, go downriver,
my life spared by luck & chance eye paddle to a poor man up in a treetop,
bad luck with him to the bitter end,
say my life spared by luck & chance on the river, eye paddle to a man in a treetop,
& him drinking bad luck to the very end,
so eye ask him; "can you make your voice a river, swim it wherever it goes?"
said, "can you turn your voice into a river, ride it to wherever it goes?
rivers carry their own rhythm brother, take you, maybe, to a better close?"
said, "rivers carry their own rhythm brother, might ride you to a better close"
he look at me, then he sang this song, "river, river, take my dreams,
carry them through my poems to sing,
river, river, carry my dreams, teach them how to swim & sing,"
sang, "let me chain my voice to you river, swim your currents to the very end,
eye say let me chain my song to you river, swim your rapids to the very end,
let me see bright day breaking through rain clouds, listen to sweet birds sing,
say let me see bright day breaking through rain clouds, hear sweet birds sing,
& sing to the bitter, bitter end

Lawd, Lawd, thank you Lawd, for letting me sing a sweet, sweet song again
Lawd, Lawd, thank you Lawd, for letting me sing a sweet, sweet song again

let me be a fish, now in your river, swimming downstream all day long,
say let me be a fish in your river Lawd, swimming downstream all day long
thank you Lawd for bringing this boy to help me get down out of this tree,
eye say thank you Lawd for bringing this boy to help me get down out this tree
my blues done taught me how to sing brand new & swim in the river, long,
say these blues done taught me to sing brand new, swim in the river, long, long
Lawd thank you Lawd, for letting me swim in this river, sing a new sweet song,
Lawd, Lawd thank you for letting me swim your river, sing a new, sweet song,
gonna pick up my old guitar today, & sing & just play along,
yes, gonna pick up my old guitar today, & sing & just play along
'cause eye chained my voice to Your river, learned to sing & swim, again
say eye chained my voice Your river, Lawd, learned to swim & sing again,
yesterday was a bitter, cold memory, but today a brighter & sweeter day.
say yesterday was a bitter, cold memory, but today is a bright, sunny day.

eye'm gonna swim my voice down this river, singing to wherever it ends,
say, gonna chain my voice to this river, Lawd, swim it to wherever it ends,
'cause eye'm a fish now in Your river, swimming downstream all day long
say eye'm a fish now in Your river, Lawd, swimming & singing all day long
my voice done took to water now like rain drops falling out of black clouds,
say my voice done took to water, like rain drops falling out storm clouds

so eye thank you my friend for help getting me out of that treetop,
now listen for my song up in the wind
say thank you my friend for talking me down out of that old treetop,
listen for my song whistling high up in the wind,
blue sky the hat eye wear now, cocked ace-duce to the singing end,
say blue sky the hat eye wear now, cocked ace-duce to the wailing end

so thank you great Lawd for letting me grow these fins & wings,
say thank you great Lawd for letting me grow these fins & wings,
& thank you friend, for helping me be myself again,
say thank you friend for bringing me Spirit, so eye can sing, again"
then he jumped into the river, began to sing & swim downriver,
say he jumped into the river, began to sing & swim downriver
eye jumped in my canoe, began to paddle upriver, going the opposite way,
say eye jumped in my canoe, began paddling upriver, in the opposite way,
while going upriver eye hear a voice singing beautiful up in the wind,
say as eye was on my way back upriver hear a sweet voice up in the wind

& eye knew it was the song the great Spirit told me eye would hear,
say eye knew it was the song the great Spirit said eye would surely hear,
so eye said;

"thank you great Lawd, for letting me walk around with this song
locked in my heart,
say thank you O Lawd for helping me walk around with a poem
locked in my heart,
that voice will be in the poems eye write & hear every day
& eye hear it strong,
say that song will be the cadence of poems eye write & hear every day
& eye hear it real strong

{ 23 }

thank you Lawd for giving me the gift to write these poems,
eye say thank you O Spirit for giving me the gift to write these poems,
for chaining my voice to a river of syllables, giving me fins & wings
for chaining my voice to a river of syllables, giving me fins & wings

thank you great Lawd, for these syllables & poems
thank you great Spirit, for these syllables & poems

eye'm gonna swim in the river of this language with my fins & wings,
& eye'm gonna swim all day long
say eye'm gonna swim in the currents of language, with my fins & wings,
say eye'm gonna swim all night long

thank you great Lawd, thank you
thank you great Spirit, thank you"

II

GRAY DAY IN JANUARY IN LA JOLLA

for Porter Sylvanus Troupe

the day absent of sun, troubles in over plush hilltops
threatening rain, cool hours mist toward noon
wearing gray shawls of vapor, patches of blue peek through
ragged holes punched in clouds, look like anxious eyes of scandinavians
worrying through their skins when they see snowstorms coming,
in a place cold & white as anything imaginable, eye look

past green foliage touched with hints of autumn shivering
like a homeless white man in a harlem doorway in february,
look past white ice storms freezing the nation, all the way to the capitol,
on martin luther king day, standing there on heated stone, bill
clinton takes his second oath of office, as rumors swirl around him
posing as vultures devouring an abandoned blood kill,

he lays out a vision for the future as good old boys dumped
like pillsbury dough into their rumpled suits fight back yawns, eyes
boring into the back of clinton's head like cold barrels of shotguns,
the cheers of the massive crowd punctuated by gun salutes,
tries beating back the cold of this day sweeping in from the arctic,
flags popping trembling wings crack over the capitol,

as jessye norman takes us where we have to go, singing:
          america, america, God shed his grace on thee, & crown thy good
with brotherhood, from sea to shining sea
but we remember the reality of ennis cosby's senseless death, on this day
out here in the west, where everything seems so cozy & warm, where
time wears the laid-back attitude of a surfer crouched on a board,

riding an incoming wave, eye see climbing up invisible ladder rungs,
deep in his imagination, the growing power of my son
porter's angular body, all arms & legs now, eyes peering out innocent
but knowing, laid-back but cold, his mind calculating the distance
his thirteen-year-old body must conquer before he understands
the meaning of roads he has just walked over pigeon-toed,

clouds breaking across tops of hillsides, light shimmying in golden
blue, the sky widening into this moment bright as anywhere
clear & warm, the voice of jessye norman touching the blues breaks through
radio, her voice evoking history washes through this poem,
implants hints of lady day's warning of "strange fruit,"
as the threat of another storm gathers itself—as love

& hatred everywhere—north of here, above san francisco,
porter & eye see shadows of clouds lengthening here in la jolla,
see them spreading down hillsides like dark amoebas, mirth,
ragged as edges of daylight slipping toward darkness,
the air cool with mist now, the hour decked out in gray shawls,
cloud vapors now puffing up into shapes of dolphins, whales,

sharks cruising a sky cold as these waters off the coastline

—1997

AMERICA'S BUSINESS: A SIMPLE PRAYER

hand over your souls & empty out all your bank accounts
for greed is one of america's main pastimes,
creating icons for this purpose, huge profits is the rule of thumb
for jesus christ superstar, marilyn monroe manson as cross-dresser,
donald duck & mickey mouse, silly little critters from disneyworld
packing them in, reducing our pulverized brains to sawdust,
daffy duck promos for big bucks, corniness rolling in liquid gold & green
backs, two-ton cartoon people trying to swim to glory through their mouths,
wearing bathing suits in shallow water, flab rolling around their midsections,
spilling over the corners of their suits like holy lard, shaking like jello
while they blather on & on like coked-up idiots, cameras rolling,
feed dream machines, while cold assistants carry duffle bags of cash to banks,
nothing spiritual here, just greed & power polished over daffiness, cornball
americana wearing blow-dried hairdos, manicured nails,
sporting attitudes of privilege, decked out in sky-blue sports
jackets with gold buttons, shiny white shoes, white socks, & a mouthful
of spit-shined, brand-new enamel—like mine—that flash brighter than day
break, than a polished, brand-new nickel, or a grinning cheshire cat,
dr. ruth spilling out rot-gut words that shoot
nails, like tails of stars disappearing over the horizon, people bailing out,
like black holes down the night, rush limbaugh lying quicker than a cobra
snake grinning happy before he strikes, but a lot of people seem
downright giddy seeing psychos get rich & famous telling them why
they should be contemplating their own wrinkled navels, wacko
talking heads, hosts swamping television air space—

the people's air space, if truth be told—get stuck on the mantra of what
they're paid to disinformation about, laughing in the silence of their brains,
pole all the way to fluctuating money markets—but y'all rich, unthinking
sapsuckers betta watch out for them hedge funds you got your money in,
hope they don't fail & pull your cardboard houses down in the doodoo
with all the rest of us unwashed zoozoos—
celebrating like crazy all over steamy airwaves,
foaming on & on as part of some nattering toothy, camera-vain,
see me now & catch me later, without regrets, pseudo punditocracy, who
dish out salacious tidbits of disinformation for everyone to take seriously,
talking loud & hard, golf tees between their teeth, so the public can't catch what
they're really talking about, O heavenly father please forgive us for not handing
over all our souls & bank accounts for all this silly bullshit, give us strength
to ward off all these murder-mouthing, greedy, power hungry, cold-blooded
hypocritical motherfuckers, save us from these vampires,
from these jesus christ superstar icons, save us from all these lucifers,
great spirit, O save us from all these spit-shined, polished, puffed up,
blow-dried hair politicians & salesmen—both the same thing—
who sell all these daffy trinkets, half-baked ideas to anyone listening,
who are trained programmers paid to raise a crowd's blood level to fever
pitch, O save us heavenly spirit before they throw the rest of us
into the cheering arena, to hungry, starving beasts for food,
like they use to, way back in italy, save us,
before glassy-eyed, gaunt lions with nothing else to do but lie trapped
inside a jerry springer styled media spectacle, who suck ragged claws,
show their blood-stained, raggedy chops, glassy-eyed,
wait for fresh lunch to be thrown in screaming,
wait for fresh meat to be thrown in screaming, every day

"SO WHAT"

miles blew "so what" on *kind of blue*
& eye do too, right here, right now,
"so what" is an attitude, a rhythm steeped & shaped,
the blues, what the cadences build then pick up,
'tudes bursting into light, high steppin it
through a room, space, where energy mimics style,
grace, the music dancing around whatever attitude brings
into the room, comes with the territory,
living in the world is not free, the beauty we receive. here,
inside this moment, is the music, is whatever we are feeling right
about now, popping our fingers as we move through a groove,
like hip people suppose to, we goose up nights,
but the space most of us cruise through is not enough
to keep the feeling real, with what we know, with what we got,
with what is brought to the table, right here, right now,

"so what" says the wind up in the music,
blowing down our lives like a tornado exploding into view,
swirling like screaming headlines, leaving false rumors all around,
faked photographs made up in dark rooms,
"so what" says ivy league assassins employed by the cia,
the government of disinformation, who drop bombs of terror
throughout our lives, who kick down our doors,
like those ski-masked bounty hunters did over in phoenix,
who blast through our dreams just because they wanted to
& could do, playing war games as if they were gods,
"so what" say the kkk of paleontologist hubris, observation,
"so what" says day-to-day bullshit dumped into our laps,
the second reconstruction is here, at our door
step, is alive & kicking, now

"so what" miles blew back in 1959,
"so what" said the tornado blowing through our lives,
"so what" say the creators of war games, doing what they do,
for the public good, freedom & democracy,
"so what" says prop 209 in california, the second reconstruction
& it was all about attitude back in 1959
& it's all about attitude, right now

IMAGE & REMEMBRANCE

on a plane ride to flagstaff, arizona,
glittering snowflakes shoot through the right wing's
beacon light, outside my window, in the night's chilling
air, streak like tracer streams of bullets,
fired from a soldier's spitting gun,
on the front line of war, anywhere

WITNESSES

the lamp posts stand mute, cold as death camp sentries,
guards the dead caught a glimpse of, just before
they gave up their last breath in volleys of spitting gunfire,
dark shades of drooping trees whispered mournfully
overhead, back then, in the chilled night air,

their leaves were serenading shadows lengthening over
the spots where the dead fell silent, as these new stones here, now,
growing up fast, posing as humans, block by block mutes everywhere,
shape the tone of fiction & friction between these ravaged buildings
popular myth holds as sacred truth, for family, community,
that we trust as love, brother & sisterhood, all that nonsense,
but where the new walking dead living here now under eaves of gables
hardly ever whisper, or pose beyond sulks, but live just to survive
this cold, silent place of bloody history & murder, red fingers
clawing graffitied walls, these dark-circled eyes those of witnesses,
are cold as cocked uzis, who have seen it all in blood & spades,
witnesses, whose eyes know the real deal beyond words,
witnesses, who know the truth going down, right now

SIGNALS & DEMARCATIONS

most times the lines are invisible as threats
eyes signaled when they flashed hate in the looks
of hitler's storm troopers in germany,
now distant cold stares in faces of well-scrubbed
apple-pie american flesh & blood images, replicated
& mailed from faraway zip codes, black christian crosses stamped
on their foreheads, most times the color of the moon (their speech
repeating in triplicate what they've heard each day from spin
doctors on radio talk shows, conservative programming,
who wave the flag in consideration for a few ducats or applause
or both—the more the merrier here—
& preach a kind of jackbooted message
the already-converted want to hear—though it strangles
the goodwill that might flow in their absence—) so very smug
in their self-ordained righteousness
they too often live behind closed minds shut air-tight,
until they unhinge like gaping mouths of mamba snakes,
& strike a horror unreal as that in cemeteries,
their laughter muted & squashed
as death of all joy in any concentration camp,
beauty stifled & stuffed into sameness of squared,
evenly cut, postage-stamp lawns, look-a-like houses
guarded by rent-an-attitude policemen in black, circling the hush
like flakes in beady-eyed cars, patrolling like clocked robots,
it is a sign of the times, of what we have come to now,
in this last gasp of this bloody century repeating itself,

before it shuts down, mass graves in bosnia and herzegovina,
genocide in ruwanda & liberia, cracking gunfire piercing innocent
skulls on brooklyn streets, razors & bombs shearing faces off
buildings, even now, in oklahoma city, tanzania, kenya, smoke
& fires curling from eyes of world trade center buildings
in manhattan, is what this century has brought us to now,
white soldiers killing blacks for spiderweb tattoos
in north carolina, the oj simpson trial
meat cleaving a grand canyon wedge between races—
as if the chasm wasn't already wide enough—
where the lines are invisible as threats
cold eyes signaled before their jackboots cracked
skulls on pavements, flashed new signs of hitler's smug
attitude, self-righteous here as bible-toting moral-
majority-christians, their voices echoing crack
white ghosts of hitler's nazis reincarnated & rubber-stamped
in lines of skinheads storm-troopering through streets,
their jackboots cracking heads all over "the land of the free"
talking about Jesus, waving guns, the american flag

—*fall 1996*

LOOKING OUT BETWEEN THINKING

eye am scoping out a lush green hillside across from me,
altogether speechless, looking out between thinking,
through a clear cool windowpane spotted with old raindrops that left
fingerprints behind, marks, what have you, blemishes, on a glass
face that reminds me of freckles, bursting, open sores festering
on this window, which might be like someone else's, who is looking at me,
right now, from the other side of the road,
their eyes zeroing in, perhaps, even as eye speak to you through
this poem, that this day might become visible, carry a syncopating, riffing
kind of line, a hipness, perhaps in pain, maybe joy, wonder, wet with rain,
somewhere eye can't even begin to speak of now but know
is there, somewhere, like my own is right here with me now

it is a kind of cosmic suffering we feel & know down deep,
though we can't put our fingers on it sometimes we still know it's there,
eye'm trying to begin speaking of it right now, here,
eye don't know why, or how, or what eye must say though whatever
eye say eye know this poem is mine, is here, right now,
because eye'm looking through it as eye speak to you,

eye feel it at this moment looking at that green hillside
across from me, which isn't exactly green—though close enough in all
its shadings to be called green—but it is shimmering, luminous, after all
this abundance of rain fell here, then went away, suddenly—
like an old raincoat you wore once suddenly up & vanished—
left behind all these glowing, green gradations,
touched with yellow or gold—& it's all about how you see things
in your own mind's eye, isn't it, like the sun shining here true enough
for me but not for others, perhaps you—touching everything gathered here,
or there, where the trees are stretching above their own waving
shadows, above the house with the built-in window,
through which someone might be looking at me right now, right here,

through their own pain—even as eye write again to you great muse, light
reflecting off the window of that suffering—across the shadows
& the road, eye am looking through my windowpane
now, looking out between thinking, seeing
that house over there built into that almost green hillside,
shimmering, touched with yellow or gold,

eye am looking through this pane of glass someone else built
through their own pain for me to watch light glancing off edges
like razors nicking flesh, lances of sunrays streaming in shadows
as the wind wags leaves of trees, leads them in a song somewhere,
other than here, winter is hinting spring & abundant rain again,
which is here right now, in winter, spring's dazzling models
beginning to try on festive clothes, one by one, a bud opening here,
a robe of geraniums there, colors of rainbows come from someplace deep
inside the earth, pop up here, then are suddenly gone like a song heard quick,
inside a moment of pure revery, where snatches of glory are caught
like a piece of beautiful fabric on a tree branch in the forest,
a sudden shimmer of voice achingly beautiful as it glides & floats,
real as a bird banking through air like a riff from *kind of blue*—
music always there filling up the distance

between looking out, thinking, holding on to whatever blooms
in that space there, polyphonic voices sluiced through interpretations
of miles measuring time traveled, from here to there,
to whatever fills the imagination up with is what we are left with, now,
is what we bring to place on the table, hold up to light for scrutiny,
this moment we are looking through as my eyes penetrate,

hold the pain eye am carrying here inside me now, a feeling
eye look through to see to the other side of the road,
where light is glancing off the window,
pain inside that house, too, built into that hillside,
almost shimmeringly green, where bold-flecked yellow heads
pop into flowers, dazzlingly burst from green bushes, whole,
lock into my vision, they are suddenly scattered there,
all over the hillside—moments sprinkled like gold

TIME LINE OF BREATH & MUSIC

for Richard Muhal Abrams

fragments blocked out in the air of a sentence,
a man on the other side of a time line
is breathing music up inside silence, is listening too,
the speech of chords riffing from top to bottom,
inside the melancholia of a moment,
back in the zone when space was caught up in the beauty
surrounding singing, the great voice anchored deep within
song, its branches running way down into the soil itself,
where the roots of trees snake their fingers down
like music branching out from different sources
to become song, to become elements of magic
climbing winged compositions of breezes,
carrying flagged newspaper pages flapping
their stingray images above, overhead, cracking
& whipping sound before they split in two, as couples do screaming—
twin birds flying in opposite directions—when they break apart
like atoms, before each fragment splits apart quick
as a note or chord sliced off the solo of a pianist's blurring fingers,
when the music block steps its way into mathematics,
pulls apart, comes back together again, is elastic

moments when breath & music kiss elusive
as mystery, the sound always shifting
the bull's-eye target, an illusion created for ears
weaves a tapestry of footsteps clopping over cobble-
stone streets, somewhere back in all that history, as here, where
a man sits high up in the gabled leaves of his imagination creating
inside a womb of silence, where a syntax of wings & breath is
translated into the language of stop & go traffic
lights, flashing divas, cornucopias shaped
like goat horns blowing out an endless supply
of edible solos, moments are sliced off like shaved glass
slivers of light, glancing off & cutting through the dark
moments of shade, like voices free-falling in time,
they lay their grids of expression over
the night or day in a time line of breath & music,
become melodies of this life that we hear & sing

TWO FOR THE PIANO PLAYERS
AT THE SPRUCE STREET FORUM

for Mike Wofford and Anthony Davis

I. MIKE WOFFORD'S SET
long-distance words peel themselves through dreams,
peal themselves like bells or wind chimes,
cascading crystal piano runs waterfalling over bosendorfer keys,
just as the fecund imagination of a solo pianist weaves a tapestry,
images sew themselves inside his tap-dancing fingers riffing out sound,
chords caressed from black & white ivory keys spool out,

along an imaginary
clothesline of sound, threads musical lines into space
& it reminds me of a piece of silk thread fed through the eye of a needle,
that tunnels through our ears, before it sews everything down, inside
the mind & heart, sitting at the apex of spirit,
where everything is calm, beauty coalesces inside touch,
the pianist hunches over his keyboard like a poet over his paper,
conjures up notes that burst sweet as cold purple grapes do
inside our mouths when they are perfectly ripe,
in season, the place green with spring or summer,
the music singing in & of itself, as fingers pull chords—
as poets pull words from someplace altogether mysterious—
in clusters that are seductive as language culled
from a place of magic, is where it all begins & ends now,
in this moment of clear seduction, the quiet is alchemized here,
is transformed by glorious sounds that are
enchanting as low purrs of lovers, their language cooing sweetness
as tongues wrapped, mysterious & bright as sunbeams teasing
touch here through slats of venetian blinds, this music clear as bars
of light slicing across shadows in a dark, dark room

II. ANTHONY DAVIS'S SET

the runs here remind me of balinese crystal geysers
spraying from waterfalls,
    here & there foaming into dissonance,
time signatures marching as time itself marches,
sound accumulating itself as it goes, car horns moving back & forth,
honking & blaring through traffic,
in manhattan, voices are also forms of accumulation,
the music here moving through space,
cutting like a razor but still
coasting, as order in chaos of times square moves through that time
as space mimicking motion but coasting anyway, revealing itself through speed
& quick change-up notions, the chameleon makeover artist there spiels
beyond what caution brings to any table
but up into symmetry anyway,
         is what it is all about here,
     nothing more or less than the sum total of rhythm,
what sound brings to our ears, our notion about the limits of artistry,
is what it is here, nothing less than energy
moving itself forward, or backward, or sideways like a sidewinder
rattlesnake, as black & white keys run disjunctive tension over themselves,
through themselves, hear everything mixed up as patois,
as mestizo, mulatto sounds, gumbo, jambalaya-american sounds
stewing in the black iron pot,
inside meltdown figures repeating themselves over & over again,
like trilling birds chirping somewhere deep inside forest-time are creating
deep magic, as in a choir of wolves mimicking thelonious monk,

their howls & yelps spraying foam as disjunctive syllables,
like after a headlong plunge through space & time a plume shaped
in the form of a feather tonguing out of the force of a waterfall hits rock,
creates music there that crescendos posthaste beyond any notion of modernity,
like deft speech does when it wears dark shades,
its words—"the bombs"—dressed up in neologic verbs & nouns
breaks into music, scats postbop like the pianist's hands bent here at the wrist,
curved fingers extended downward like long graceful necks of feeding swans,
turn into legs that tiptoe over keyboards like sleuths
moving through space with the beauty of bojangles robinson, & we watch
the pianist's fingers flashing over the black & white ivory keys in a blur,
hear the leapfrogging magic spewing mystery up into chords that echo
like birdcalls once heard in a munich english flower garden,
hear the ear-popping runs of art tatum here, the music transporting,
like a great meal washed down smooth with a great bottle of wine,
the moment here alchemistic, alcheringa, in the end, pure magic

TEMPUS FUGIT/C.T.A.

for Miles Davis, Bud Powell, & Jimmy Heath

the music moving through speakers in waves,
hip, on the money, voices from the past
insinuate, probe, break down cool into hot slinky
language moving in tempo above the beat,
inside the beat, behind it, solos pop,
build the tension, a man in bop time scats,
runs down time signatures in blue-bop-post-bop lines,
time humps beneath hard driving, glittering, new, slick
musical surfaces, scatological
phrasing sluices in sweet, new, understated tones,
but on top of the tempo, in time with the time,
is where the music goes, wearing dap, new clothes,
faces mirrored in time changes, musical signatures,
the ebb & flow of exchanges underneath it all,
inside the music, tension building there
as in a volcano about to explode,
the music, like thick lava flows new, hot,
smokes until it cools, hardens & adds on,
extends whatever was there before it came new
cruising through, smoothing down edgy bebop,
the blues underneath it all voiced slickly,
new as the language sluicing from the beats,
new as a language bursting from a nation

SYNCHRONICITY IN BOLOGNA, ITALY

for Jeff Biggers & Bill Demby

a sweet day strolling light here, breaking through breeze-licked
cool shadows, under terra-cotta porticoes, the sky up in the gables
streaked blue, where light plays off burnt sienna barriers that stand there
soft as moss clues in your eyeballs, as chewed-off red & ochre language flakes
here warm as bolognese spaghetti sauce, my sight leaps vertigo, all hues
held aloft here splash & dash through old walls all soft & warm too,
as caribbean seas lapping green-blue waters are filled with heat of lovers,
your eyeballs tongue honey-toned thighs of marvelously shaped women,
who are high-stepping it through these moments

                                      clear as church bells ringing
                                              in the town
squares of hip bologna
       & we are seduced by the architecture here older than these words
sluicing through passageways, skirts of prancing young fine things flicking up
their switching beauty at the hemlines, reveal bodies
firmer than ripe grapes—& juicier, too—than sweet oranges on the vine—
hello—as they burst through time quicker than music heard here in castaneting
heels that bind the old to the bold, offered up as proof in footsteps that dance
behind you as we swivel our heads—readers—
catch a glimpse of a blur moving at the speed of sound & beauty,
mystery breaking through these moments like syllables flashing across
our view like saxophone, trumpet, or piano solos laced with silver, guitar sounds
breaking down here like jimi hendrix—& eye know it's all too hard to describe
or put together here, in a sentence—
how to appreciate it all, these glorious bodies swinging
like great solos jumping out of faces, dew-damp old buildings, doors,
what can be said but that they are marvelously sculptured clues racing through

the minds of those who live here now, or those like me, who are passing through,
who perhaps resemble this man, who looks like a sheep's eye of a bedouin, who is passing
me now & who might perhaps think americans cheap
& bittersweet as coca-colas,

his prickly black beard dusted with specks the color of cocaine,
his face serene as the truth george washington once told recounting cutting down
that mythical tree, the day here smelling of great food—as all the days here do—riding
a breeze that turns quickly on a dime—like a pirouette—it doubles back
to lick your face, coolly as you climb your spirit up the winding green road
that leads straight up to the top of the mountain,
a cool drink like a poem washing down your imagination,
                                                    roses & bougainvilleas
brightening up the tonguing, sweet air surrounding you,
as two rows of cypresses, straight as candle flames
                                        shoot skyward,
guard the road like sentries at the medieval castella de la romena,
south of bologna, in the appenini hills, where dante wrote
the thirty-first canto, north of vollombrosa
where milton wrote *paradise lost,*
                            above the devil's church,
where the monk fleeing the devil fell to his death screaming through
pure mountain air cold as a hawk diving down death on a prey,
on a day clear & perfumed as this one perhaps, as the valley rolls out below
like a rug full of patches of roasted barley & wheat,
their tops waving like elongated spiked heads of punk
rockers, in fields in sight of bartizans

& the old way of life rules supreme here still

outside of bologna, vollombrosa,
castella de la romena with its bartizan turrets, no plastic, or neon
culture ruling here, but architecture 800 years old,
& people carrying tradition in their moist olive eyes—

& who walk in a slow, measured gait in the countryside—

& where time is measured out by the number of breaths
one takes in, breathes out, afternoons wafting through lyrical here
as whispering flutes that become bassoons when dark fierce storms roll through,
their breath stabbed by cracking lightning bolts,

time leaving its mark on everything everywhere here,
in voices long gone but rustling still amongst trembling leaves of trees,
who speak to you during ghost moments after midnight,
speak to you too with joy, burnished as sienna walls

dusted with clues at the first crack of daybreak

ROBERT COLESCOTT'S "ONE-TWO PUNCH" AT THE VENICE BEINALE

I.

before anything else, at the first crack of day
light, prowling around your studio,
during the hush hours after midnight, in the dry air
surrounding the desert where you live, a stone's throw
outside of tucson—obelisks of cactus standing tall
guarding the entrance to your sanctuary—
the first thing you do when you approach the white canvas,
stretched four-corner-square before you on a huge white wall,
is paint the surface bright red after thinking about it for days—
the tug & pull of your brushstrokes over the surface creates
swirling shapes of music that move in & out of themselves,
magical shapes that are mysterious backdrops
for paradoxes about to become known,
roiling at the point of birth, inside the womb of your canvas—
red shapes that seem to burst & boil over their seams
hot as volcanic lava flows, boiling & roiling
red underneath its own skin of flames,
red as blood pulsating through veins underneath skin,
at the point of creation, the muse lifting the idea—
an embryo—that will evolve into something
within a canvas—a womb filled with blood?—
painted bright red, your adrenaline flowing now, colescott,
flowing onto the surface through your refiguring brain
birthing the idea, layer after layer of colors swirling through
the snapshot you have taken inside your head of what
you are about to do here, whatever comes to you,
like improvised music, will find its way up there,
stroked as images upon your sea of red primer,
where what the viewer first sees will provoke "humor,"
then "pleasure," before fast becoming a "problem"

II.

shapes emerging as color fields take on form, break through
the surface of red primer that is a womb filled with blood,
a letter from yourself to yourself, a conversation if you will,
here & there bodies lump down grotesquely under faces,
primeval in their distortion, blotchy with earth tones that shock
the senses, pulled in & appalled by what they think they see here,
at first glance, lumpy body shapes of brown & black & white
touched with hints of pink & yellow look bawdy,
as caricatures, demons cut loose from a bad dream swirl,
point guns out at the viewer from your canvases, colescott,
a doctor holding a hypodermic needle stands
next to a priest holding a severed black head, two gorillas
stabbing another, a skeleton with a green head leers off to the side,
red chains around a wrist in a painting invaded with orange crabs,
a tale of gumbo spilling out of a black woman's mouth, a pig
in the corner, a cup of coffee perched on her nose,
the hunchback of notre dame in blackface moons inside a circle holding a blonde,
next to a white something cannibalizing
a black man's body, over a black football player,
the "death of the old mulatta," chains & guns in saudi arabia,
jesus contemplating the world for lunch as a golden hamburger,
black slaves, chained to tree trunks blooming
cotton candy leaves that hold maps of the new world & europe,
look like red-lipped monkeys or gorillas in front of a pile of bananas & corn, while
somewhere else a silver choctaw nickel holds
a half-breed negro smoking a cigar, whimsy,
as gorillas & mulattas do the tango a rogue white bilingual cop
speaking out both sides of his mouth, castigates
a mexican & black man drunk on sleep amongst skulls,
rats, & garbage, cactuses growing from ghettos of rock & sand—
broken-down dreams, is that how they choose to see us, colescott—
as a man behind a crumbling wall of redbrick threatens,
firepower in his hand, a raised black nightstick about to back up
the badge on his chest, spitting invectives & realism

III.

& what are we to make of these besotted, misbehaving figures—
lumpy shapes of clay posing as humans—colescott,
their actions mirroring what we see & do each & every day,
are we to go beyond the tough aesthetics rendered here, gloating
idiots bamboozling the senses, what we think & know of ourselves,
cloned here, pretenses stamped into our heads as cartoons
we grow ourselves into, caricatures of popular culture
you turn on their heads through parody, skewed standards of beauty pierced by
your cryptic social commentary, myth, allegory imploded,
symbols of religion turned upside down on their heads, crudeness,
biting satire are messages you send to yourself mapping fears
you hold, "frustration & anger," communicated through madcap, "sophisticated
literary illusions," rendered lush in lavish colors, through painted narratives you
reveal the mongrel history—
"the interconnectedness" between races, power manipulated
when "standards" are controlled, beauty arbitrarily stolen
from "the eyes of the beholder,"—& tell us africa is "a source
of life"—black artists here in america the avant-garde cutting edge—
& it's a subversive agenda you're working here, colescott,
"the art of irony" suffusing everything you do, exaggerated manners, distortions,
reversal of images brought down to us through history,
"silly white invention" laid down on us as truth,
& eye see music in your paintings, colescott, rhythm & mastery,
your own way of viewing truth, magic as surprise, things revealed once we have
gone inside & looked beyond the archetypal images
you paint deep down inside content, what has evolved over time,
life viewed through white eyes & black eyes, too,
there, up on your canvases, the world revealed in glorious colors, narratives
that allow us to walk right through an "open door,"
to enter the freedom of your expression in astonishment we hear
the music of duke ellington & miles davis jumping right out
of your paintings, white brown black red faces tinged with pink
& yellow, races transmogrified through reversals of history—
blonde & black lumpy figures of clay posing as humans

SIGHTING BIRDS AT THE BEACH

I. FLYING FISHERBIRDS

joined together behind the asshole nexus of a leader
two v-shaped lines of pelicans cruise overhead
in la jolla, winged fisherbirds headed out
into the boiling gray mist of a fog
foaming in from the pacific
on the downside of a
late but early
autumn
afternoon in
september, their cookie-
cutter bodies punching out irregular
black holes & shapes up there in space on a day
gray as sadness, these anglers gliding by like fighter planes
riding currents of wind & light, turning as they fly by in formation
their necks craning upward, straining outward—like wings slightly bent at
the tip—& downward (like cockpit cabins of concorde jets raising
lickety-split, hell-bent for europe) they rise up scanning
the rolling roiling waves, looking down beady-eyed
avengers scooping up fish from waving
water there—pelicans following
their spearheaded leader—
fisherbirds
tracking new skies
over boundless salt seas rancid
with the death-flesh odor of countless
entombed there—but a table of food stretching out
in front of a pelican's keen vision—wings spread wide to
catch a ride on sweet breaths of looping breezes there, totipalmates
webbed feet tucked underneath, like airplane wheels right after takeoff
their distensible pouch bills empty which drives them to dip
& glide ever alert eyes zeroing into curling waves for possible
kills, like heat-seeking radar one leaves the v-shaped
formation—knife blade plunging toward
the sea's heart—O pelican diving
O pelican—deep sea
fisherbird

II. GRACEFUL SCAVENGERS

on the ground, seagulls wobble around beaches
like drunken, beady-eyed judges
without their black robes on, stepping stiff-legged across
sands dirty as the colors of their feathers
snatching food from the mouths of bawling toddlers
with their long, rapier-like beaks, they peck at beer cans,
styrofoam cups—anything they see, really—leaving webbed
birdprints tracking through sand, they look sideways out of mean
red eyes, wobbling about on toothpick legs, they wobble top-heavy
fat bodies around like black church deacons
or plump wall street executives, shuffling herky-jerky
side-to-side, their demeanor that of solemn funeral home directors
heads up, eyes alert for scraps of anything thought to be edible
their beaks jackhammering the earth as they strut by, gray-white
pilfering birds, so wretched down here on the ground
but lawd so beautiful cruising up there in space—
like anything the imagination thought was graceful or sleek—
easing in & out of wind currents, they bank & glide, float
& climb like a great idea spotlighted in prime time

WHENEVER EYE WALK BY

whenever eye walk by now
sometimes men & women jump
startled out their skins
whenever
they hear the sound
of my new knee
brace squeaking—unoiled
steel rubbing up against steel
beneath foam
rubber—

perhaps they're
                    thinking,
whenever they hear that
squeaking sound:

there's a beady-eyed
mouse, in the house,

somewhere

STYLE IS

style is bebop, cool jazz slick strolling
words phrased through space in a blue span
of time, is hip-hop, rap, & attitude cruising
a deep way of thinking rooted in a stance, is a man,
or a woman, dressed to fashion plate perfection,
their clothes hung just so,
"clean" as a miles davis muted solo,
they strut their sweet stuff blooming cologne
& perfume behind them, are wrapped inside a bearing,
good taste trailing like fresh waterfalls, their voices
cascades of honeyed syllables sing like morning
birds, or breezes licking silver tongues,
kissed through shivering wind chimes

MOTHER

for Dorothy Smith Marshall

when eye was growing up she used to sit in the bathroom, each & every
morning, smoking kool cigarettes, drinking hot coffee, reading newspapers,
a hard toilet seat caressing her derriere, reading glasses in place,
serious as cancer, the way her eyes devoured everything,
finished old newspapers stacked up high as her waistline when she stood
proud, erect, defiant, all of five feet two inches tall in high heel shoes, petite,
she was a pistol when she was young, eyes blazing, boring in
like bullets when her temper squeezed the trigger of her ire
hard, her rage angry scars she raised on me & my brother's backs & legs,
dealt out with ironing cords that hissed through the air like whips, coiled snakes
about to strike, it was her mother's influence (she was scared to death of her
mother—mama to me & my brother timmy—), who believed in retribution,
payback, fear, to the bitter end we watched mama slap mother around hard,
once or twice, for some perceived transgression, or indiscretion,
but we loved them both deeper than fear itself,
loved mother, mama too, because we knew we were a lot to handle—
my brother & me—born to do mischief in a neighborhood full of young thieves,
malcontents, murderers-to-be, you name it, they thrived & flourished there—
the good & straight we rejected out of hand as past tense, negro, square
as blocks we played with once until we wrapped hands around straight razors—
so she cracked the whip hard, raised welts on our backs & hardening butts,
legs & arms, kept fear alive in us, to keep us in line, & alive

she always had books around the house, introduced me to poetry & novels,
wanted to be a schoolteacher, raising me & my brother got in the way of that
& as she grew older she left a string of glassy-eyed suitors
in her wake, my father being the first who didn't make it all the way
home, where her sweet perfume trailed through the air like flowers
blooming fresh in springtime, gardenias of lady day, sometimes
jasmine, or roses, it depended on her mood, but there was always something
about her that kept them coming back for more, time & again,
whatever she had bewitched them with, her charm, maybe,
that could be as dazzling as the smile flashing above her sensuous walk
that beckoned, her step so light she seemed to float through air, meriny-yellow
in skin tone, plum, cushiony lips, splashed bright red & full, smooth,
she called herself a party girl—though she was always much more than this,
though she was this, too—with a great sense of style, dressed to kill cock-
robin, could press pedal to the metal out on the dance floor,
she caused heads to swivel on necks like spinning tops,
whenever she passed, her fragrance tantalizing nostrils,
trailing behind her like a sweet-smelling, invisible plume

she's in her eighties now, still sits on the toilet stool each & every morning,
repeating the same ritual, only now she doesn't smoke anymore,
everybody's gone to the other side on her side of the family—mama,
her brothers garfield & allen, aunts & uncles, cousins, her daddy, mine too—
men her age still sniff behind her glassy-eyed, whenever she honors them
when she looks their way, still a fashion plate, the best of her time, her smile
remains dazzling, her skill to squeeze copper from a penny, squirrel away
money—a survivor of the depression, she is tenacious—for rainy days,
she's softer now, tells me she loves me every time we speak
over the telephone, tells me, with regret, she could have done better by me,
but that's hogwash, because she did the best she could with what she had,
& that was more than enough to get us through all the madness,
she is still a pistol at 81, has all of her real teeth, too, has outlived all her
suitors, except this last one, biff, who, she says, is slowing down at 79,
she still walks with a bounce in her stride, seems to still float across
& through the air, her eyes blazing bore in on you still like bullets
whenever she squeezes the trigger of her hot temper, ire
& eye love her more than eye could ever imagine,
love her far deeper than fear itself

THE SILVER FLOWER IN BILBAO

for Frank O. Gehry, Architect & Artist

a silver flower has bloomed
by the river in bilbao,
the guggenheim has sprouted whole,
shaped its curved titanium skin into petals
that catch streaking bolts of lightning
flashes shimmering with waves
of gold, then orange, red
when the sun drops
through sunset
like a gold coin

a work of art this building,
angles thrusting like whale snouts,
or the bows of ships easing out to sea,
the image stamped into a reflecting pool
is bold, a remarkable sculpture piece,
its huge glass walls bring in
the city, daylight,
the river curving around
like some huge anaconda snake
slipping out to sea, its gray skin

flecked by mica-bits of glittering
light, sparkles intensely as the flower's
titanium skin, in the wee-small hours,
before & after midnight,
when the sky's skin is dark,

the moon's smile is galvanizing

JEREZ DE LA FRONTERA
for Peter

I.

in the deep black hours of jerez, after midnight, margaret is a mummy
wrapped in a white sheet where she sleeps, in the dead of night, she lies
in the center of our bed, stiff as demeanors of some european aristocrats, peter,
your house quiet as church mice sniffing gold leaf pages of a book of sacrament,
a cool breeze licking in over white walls & slanted roofs from the east filters
heat, announces morning light is not far off, wedded, as it is, to daybreak, soon
the white bridal gown of first light will spread out its hem, lift its white lace
veil, while a lengthening train of clues breaks the dark into spreading
blues, which are current everywhere, common as the lyrics of muddy waters,
john lee hooker, lightnin' hopkins, somewhere deep inside
a snoring voice of lament breaks through the last vestiges of quiet hours,
at the center of a slippery moment full of dreaming, a motorbike zips through,
leaning around corners, it escalates the language of its speed as it shoots, veers,
clues itself into somewhere it is due, gearing down toward silence as it blows
past white walls & roofs collaged in bold relief against a spangled black sky,
they look like still lifes from my second-floor window over the garden,
while margaret's sweet fragrance rises like seduction from where she sleeps,
her body a stand-in for a mummy wrapped in white linen, her face sweet,
is turned toward the window as if to kiss first light when it comes

II.

now a sliver of moon smiles through our room above the tiny chimneys,
they seem to wear small hats cocked ace-duce, like the icon of tio pepe sherry,
peter has told us of the burning hot wind of dust & fire called la vente,
which brings grief from the east, when the weather vane's arrow head points
in the direction of seville, granada's alhambra, lorca's moorish part of andalusia,
its craggy mountain peaks sharp as alligator teeth, their skin the color of chalk
brown mixed with ochre, greens, reds, white villages & towns—
& one the shape of one of miró's floating birds—sweep across this heat-
stricken landscape of late august, up & down rolling, warbled landscapes,
rendered mysterious by el greco's surreal, strangely beautiful canvases,
they seem to be rising up from some moonscape, somber dream,

but today the weather vane arrows north, toward madrid & morning
breaks through smells of coffee, footsteps that crack hard as castanets, or skulls
being popped open when smashed against old cobblestone streets, spilled brandy
that stained tiled squares checkerboarding the walkway of the plaza plateros
last night, is being washed clean, right before daylight breaks apart my dreams,
eye hear in the center of my imagination the roar of a bullring, erupting
cheers in the arena roll up & down, a cadence of emotive conundrum,
& in the middle of it all eye feel the matador slaying the bull,
in the center of the arena, see its blood flowing bright as the matador's red suit,
emblazoned with golden epaulets, hear in my mind's ear clapping castanets,
cracking sounds of flamenco dancers shoes slapping the floor staccato,
in a rhythm reminding me of popping sounds of conga drums, miles' lamenting
trumpet on *Sketches of Spain,* now that the sun is high in the blue eye follow
the curve of his mournful lament, fully awake now, walk down
to your walled-in courtyard peter, bright with green, yellow chumbera cactus
buds, bright birds of paradise shoot out blooming tongues that burst into heads,
geraniums fragrant as the sparkling water fountain is lyrical, tantalize
the senses, you want to sit here forever amongst these red & yellow lobster
claws, scarlet red begonias laddering, emblazoning these old walls,
want to sit & write poems of hope & serenity, but today, back in the states,

president clinton is being deposed in front of a grand jury, people screaming
his head be axed off, thrown into a bucket like fish, or snakes

but you wring out words of joy, peter, they roll off your tongue lyrical
as a happy mantra, relieved the weather vane's arrowhead still points north,
the breeze tongue cool as springs of water high in mountains of italy,
you are relieved the day is not scorching hot with la vente,
though we hear words circling the american congress like declarations of war,
on that day we would go down to the beach between cádiz & rota,
where the waves washing in rough & warm were beautiful, the sun setting low,
in the west, just before evening wrapped itself around us like the arms
of a favorite relative, my spirit reaching out across the straits of gibraltar felt
the tip of africa, so close, so far away, the promontory of cádiz pointing
like a finger full of white buildings toward the dark continent,
when the light grew dark as the sun dropped like a ripe orange into the sea,
where ships crawled into port like giant bugs, sea gulls glided over & through
the sweet, cool air, like toy planes banking over waves thick as molasses,
the air here thick with andalusian spanish, syllables cracking rapid fire,
machine-gun staccato, the laughter sudden as terrorist explosions,
spontaneous as great music is always, everywhere it is played

III.

night has come again to this place of caballos, noble horses & brave fighting
bulls with curved horns trying to kill a matador with a red cape,
toro, toro, toro, bravo, toro, the cheers rise as the bloody black bull charges,
toro, toro, toro, a man & a red cape & a horse, the spectacle beyond what
eye feel is beauty, though eye see there in movement the sheer power,
choreography of war, the grace of man & beast during a moment
at the edge of death, locked into a mode of survival, is as far as my heart can go
in the service of destruction for beauty, who am eye to say what is or isn't glory,
the lance poised in the air like a scorpion's tail before the strike is art for so many,
murder to others, in this land of the inquisition & franco's execution of lorca,
what is there to know but your own heartbeat pulsing love, peter,
the blood of friendship pure as your smile or hug, these bodegas of wine you have shared
peter, full of the finest sherry, meals scarfed down & laughter shattering moments
like gunfire, these are the things you remember, castanets & flamenco dancers,
the chimneys cocked ace-duce like icons of tio pepe in the cool evenings,
your gracious, spontaneous smile, my friend, your friendship brought us here,
for me to see margaret's body wrapped like a mummy in lacy white linen,
asleep in the center of our bed, the shades open, in the dead of fragrant nights,
her face sweet, always turned toward the open window, as if to kiss
the first morning light when it comes, is a blessing & a gift,
eye tell you now, peter, it is a blessing & a rare, poetic gift

—*summer 1998*

III

THE POINT LOMA POEMS

THE POINT LOMA POEMS:
WRITTEN FOR THE WASTEWATER MANAGEMENT PROJECT
for the Sculptor, Mathieu Gregoire, who got me involved

I.

reader, let your painterly imagination run true as a brushstroke,
straight out to sea, let your eyes zoom along a single line
curving away from this artificial walkway & barrier,
this cliff of sand, clumps of grass, large & small boulders, look
out toward the horizon, where blue meets blue on a clear day,
where a bar of mist separates the two, the view expansive everywhere
from here, the blue sky spreading soft lips of air to kiss the many
feverish mouths of fish opening & closing out in the pacific,
where desire is a need to hold all this power in check,

where that straight line you pull yourself out by now holds true,
on course, your eyes drinking in everything your mind can swallow,
there, where the mouth that holds the tongue that speaks
in breaking syllables, with foaming articulation, roaring in in one curling wave
after another, suds at the point of apogee, like a madman stunned by a miracle
when he looks out, sees a single color between green & violet meet
each other as lovers fuse at the point where the sun touches their flesh,
at each place along their line of connection, we are fascinated by it all,
when light fades toward alchemy, the power deeply magical here,
mysterious as touch when it seduces flesh, where true colors fade into gradual
gradations, the palette swelling with cool heat of blues where your vision leaps
out now reader, to embrace the glow that holds the line
true from this point forward, now

reach out your ears & senses toward titillation, stretch them out,
listen to, feel the music re-creating itself out there where the sun refracts
its lancing rays that multiply into a billion slivers of light that cut
& sparkle like diamonds on the back of this blue ocean, a miracle
spread out like an endless azure veranda (table toward which pelicans & sea-
gulls dive, swoop over & feed on squawking & barking like hungry sea lions
everywhere on wet, black rocks), the language of a poem that suddenly grows

wings, takes off in flight, reaches this place here where sea, land, & sky meet
light, at the end of point loma, beneath a slope of scrub bush, bright magenta
ice plants & pickle, now let your mind rest here, space traveler,
where weeds climb these hillsides of green & rough brown
rocks—now a grave from where four dooky flames used to shoot
orange lizard tongues rippling skyward, miraging air with heat,
waves that whales use to navigate themselves in by,
after crossing the pacific, geysering up spray foam jets from holes
in their backs, drench with saltwater where waves curl, form patterns
way out in the humping mad waves locked like lovers,
waves moving up & down like a chain of U's, curving question marks, way up
above poseidon holding his three-pronged fork, who can cause earthquakes
to lift the towering water higher until it breaks & dives down smashing
against the surface/skin, it becomes a boiling cauldron there,

imagine yourself in that boiling cauldron of curling power, reader,
a whale or a surfer or eyes from a boat looking back at this stunning
land, rising as if it were the outer walls of a bowl seen from here as a backdrop,
the sea floor curving up to meet it, form the highest rim, imagine stunned reader,
it is the golden hour of seven in the evening, you are riding a wave in,
it's summer & a bar of sunlight wrinkles & ripples across the surface of waves
as they wash in before disintegrating as foam on the shining black rocks,
now imagine this: you are a surfer & the same ray of sunlight behind your head
casts a light that reflects off your surfboard onto the waves,
you think you're looking into a mirror, then a halo circles around
your body as you ride the imploding power cruising toward extinction,

look now & see the vortex, reader, swelling around rocks before you
like rings around jupiter, where brown kelp swims tangled as nests of snakes
inside tidepools, swirling inside mouths of yawning caves next to wet black
rock islands holding shimmering seals
washed bright as black babies' shiny bottoms, wet with pee,
the air here smelling of salt, waves crashing in carrying the power
& language of tornadoes howling like runaway trains,

still there is a feeling of calmness where you stand looking out through
pelting mist, waves slobbering fringes of lace exhaust themselves
like madmen in eddying, swirling shapes,
in this tide pool where you stand just now, reader, you are
following these words to the land's end to watch them disappear,
only to appear somewhere else, perhaps right around the corner,
like waves & currents at the end of another journey

II.

& now you find yourself back here again before your eyes
& mind began to roam, again, before you imagined yourself out there
in all that power looking in, the air here smelling of bromide,
mixed with the sharp odor of garbage,
now you stand here again reading these lines
before moving down the granite path parallel to the tide pool, the land's end
& wherever you go now the smell of humankind is everywhere—
after all, each san diegan leaves a little piece of themselves
out here, a piece of memory, soiled plastic gloves, condoms, chewing gum,
their wrappers glinting in kidneys of pulverized dogs, smashed tin cans,
some leftover potatoes gone to goo, a lost diamond ring, perhaps,
a coin swirled down a toilet stool with that stinking eel-like long stuff that slides
soft as a snake from someone's derriere, a blitzkrieg of snails crushed beyond
whatever your recognition can handle, after a rainstorm, something
sharp as a blade of glass, a steel pitcher, a crab, a seashell,
a cornucopia of anything imaginable ends up out here—
at the end of point loma, gathered in a truly democratic state,
inside lakes full of ferric chloride, anionic polymer,
inside gigantic sed-tanks armed with aluminum teeth,
all carried here by cutthroat or parsifal flumes
that separate liquids from solids that fall to the bottom of tanks,
there to be scraped to one end to become sludge matter
pumped into digestors, it is cooked as food is inside stomachs,
turned into gases & transformed into electricity that runs everything
here on point loma, the liquid pumped through rainbows of underground pipes,

sluicing & rushing with the sound of pulverizing floods, it zooms itself out
through dusty tunnels of concrete & steel, is shot out
quick as a blink into the pacific,
shot way out through a gigantic high-powered gun,
whose trigger is forever being pulled

III.

wastewater becomes a tongue of speech that commingles
inside that dark shadowy world where denizens of the deep
sleep, where life is cold & cheap & heights & depths are sheer
& steep, where long-lost secrets keep cold in heaps of stones, rest
side by side with bones, where above it all, in the brimming sunlight,
swimmers & dolphins skim, break the surface carried by waves,
where you see yourself now, reader & traveler, memorizing a place
where you throw your vision out to again, somewhere,
at the point where sea meets sky, the color there somewhere in between
green & violet, a warm sun touching that place with affection,
as in the seduction you, too, feel now, when you allow your mind to open
as a flower grown here in this barren place of great beauty, bloom,
like life anywhere breath is taken, the moment here cherished,
embraced as creation shaped by love, what it is before you now,
here, at the land's end, the color somewhere in between
green & violet, where the sea meets the sky,
where the sea is married to the sky

IV.

a long winding road takes you away from this place
of humming machines & low concrete buildings,
side by side with hot pink bougainvilleas, slow sounds of men
pile-driving stones in hard hats below chattering helicopters
hovering in patrol just off shore, at the land's end, danger in high
voltage wires popping & snapping warning signs everywhere,
hissing messages in black lettering against canary yellow, chipped black
on white, beige against brown, a mirror checking you out as you pass,
everywhere dusted with fine chalk here,

a kind of institutional sameness, now leave all that behind
& move out down this snaking path, pass a parking lot out beyond the hum
of men & machines struggling to leave their mark on destiny & control,
where the land ends, forms the head of a sea otter,
its body the cliff wall falling away to the rocks below, where
waves crash spending their hissing language of frilly lace,
like breath of people back out in the real world,
the beauty of this place & the sea stretching out here
in front of your eyes, your imagination carrying you
anywhere you want to, on a gray day even, cuddling inside
the sweetness of your lover's almond-shaped eyes that speak to you
now, so seductively here, inside your head when that voice whispers
your name sweet as anything you could ever imagine,

so smile when you think of love blooming as a flower,
watching the freedom of a seagull soaring above everything,
these walls where you can read these words, come closer,
don't ever be afraid of these words,
come closer, rub your mind up against them as you stroll this path,
turn them over like they are good food inside your brain,
chew on them, treat them as if they were long-lost friends come back
to visit you, here, dropped in from anywhere,
they won't hurt you, now watch them as they move as flight,
as birds spreading wings & climbing skyward,
across the pages of your mind,
toward the sun, think of them as freedom, my friend,
as sprung from a dream, the future in this seagull
perched on this wall hit by sunlight,
think of these words as guides, new-found friends
as you walk out in all this glorious air & light here,
feel the wind's tongue rubbing up against your scrubbed face,
the music of the waves crashing & roaring like a lover's climax
when they hit rocks & you'll know freedom there,
rough & cold & late, but still beautiful,
yes, think of these words as keys to freedom my friend,
syllables that are keys unlocking doorways to freedom,
that lead you along this north nature path,

yes, think of them as freedom, friend,
savor these words here at the land's end,
that is shaped like a sea otter's head

     V.

& the sea otter's head connects the path that leads us
up the backside of this windswept place, the path winding
higher & higher, swinging up & bending around
this barren spot like an elongated L, or a boomerang slicing
behind eight digestors that serve as stomachs,
scrub brush squatting on hillsides sloping up or down—
whatever your perspective—thorn bushes
wedged into rock & dirt, wind & birds waltzing at your back
disguised as mozart or bach, what you hear inside your head now
is what you evoke there hiking this east slope nature path,
the rim of the hill above you quilting
colors of various browns & greens, beethoven's music
playing dramatic in the thundering swells bursting against rocks,
& when you look out at the pacific from here you can see
beyond what you saw before when you were down there,
amongst the low sounds of electricity humming, mixed with jackhammering,
hard-hatted men (who probably listen to music of elvis or country & western—
maybe you, too, reader, or perhaps miles davis, tupac shakur,
duke ellington, or U2), your mind running out in front of you now,
or resting in meditation, awestruck by what you see out in all that blue,
the view stretching out from yourself to embrace the humpback
coronado islands off of baja, planes arrowing skyward from lindbergh field,
helicopters split in half by rays of light from the sun, clouds cruising away fast
as some promises made by politicians, on a clear day

the possibility of seduction by what you see here is everywhere
around you, as you trip the light fandango, play off
the waves that dance & swell, you hear the sound of castanets
in your head, see the licking light moving up the magenta slope
as the sun goes down, click by click, as if it were measured by a clock
inside God's head, the movement now from bright glare

to lengthening shadows with every click,
& with every click waves climb higher up walls,
leave seashells in tidewater basins looking like white skulls
from here, as the sun drops golden, click by click, its legacy is its light
reaching out a long orange arm across the darkening water to touch
you here, reader, where you stand or move along & through
this pathway of rock & gravel, this thicket of turning pages,
below the rim of this hill time stretching out before you now
(an act of possibility or love?), as the sky turns orange-
gold, just before twilight, you embrace beauty where you are
reader, embrace the highest possibility of yourself, right now,
at this moment, embrace the parameters of an idea,
whose time has come, is singing here, right now

THE POINT LOMA SERIES OF HAIKUS & TANKAS

for Mathieu Gregoire

I.

beauty all places
here, look inside yourself now,
look deeper, it's there

II.

gray day underground
in the tunnel, bright, warm sun
outside in the blue,
inside your own deep working
time, thoughts of making sweet love

III.

think of making love
to the work that you do here,
think of it as song,
music whispering, a breeze,
a tongue of someone you love

IV.

think of a sweet place,
now that you are here, in all
this darkness, light where
you are standing with yourself,
wherever you have to go

v.

smile whenever you
think of the sweet love blooming
inside your hard head,
think of it as a flower
you will hand to someone soon

vi.

down here in darkness
think of roses when you look
at these concrete walls

vii.

your mind a window
to look inside yourself, see
a rich garden there,
bright with flowers, whose faces
pop the air like sweet music

viii.

deep rumblings in air,
is sound of sea waves smashing
skulls of wet black rocks

ix.

somewhere on a hill
burning candle flames—tall pines
shoot up, reach skyward,
their v, for victory, signs—
lick hot tongues, scorch the air

YOUR LOVER'S EYES SPEAK

your lover's eyes speak
to you so softly in this
place of wind, sea, bright blue sky,
sunlight after the gray lifts,
stuns your face into smiling

JUST BENEATH THE PROMONTORY

just beneath the promontory
the pacific is ebbing & flowing
in & out, in waves
like the push & pull of bodies,
lovers breathing in & out,
engaged in their work,
their pleasure

COME CLOSER

come closer, don't be afraid of these words,
come closer, rub your mind up against them,
see in them the possibility that birds seek,
like ones perched on the other side of this wall
& further out to see where the waves crash,
aren't they beautiful there dressed all in black
& white feathers, like some skin-tones, look, see
them in their flocks there in the sun shaking off
water sprays from their feathers, now their wings
opening & closing before they take flight to freedom,
as sea waves crash in in foaming thunder leaving
their lace hissing at the top of their curling flight,
crashing, then eddying back out as spent bubbles,
look at all this evoked in the words of this poem,
isn't it beautiful, the view seen from here
my friend, on this dark wall leading up
to snatch a little sunlight at the end of this
tunnel, my friend, dig down & find the light
within yourself, see that seagull there ready
to take flight, as if sprung from a dream, there
as you walk out this dark tunnel into the glorious
air & light, you hear waves crashing their thunder
as the seagull takes flight, you know freedom's
out there, at the end of these words

IV

BROKEN IN PARTS:
A HEALING SONG FOR SAXOPHONE & VOICE

for Oliver Lake & Kwame Ture (Stokely Carmichael) 1941 – 1998

I.

broken in parts, broken in parts, the earth fractured & fissured
is broken in parts, voices censored, broken off in space,
in their place the silent ooze of breathing, pulsating between worlds
between place parts of syntax floating on surfaces of speech like islands
floating in the middle of rivers, in the middle of nowhere & everywhere
    zigzagging omens waving flags of menace like flapping tongues,
everything seemingly coming apart in a sea of wreckage,
someone is drowning we don't hear or see,
threads suddenly gone, clues, beliefs
suddenly torn asunder by sawblading teeth, hemorrhaging
blue-meanies shooting through dreams after winds blew buzz saw glass
through dazed wonder, life chewed up between jackhammering jaws,
as a razor cuts through a living tongue & it is bleeding
speech cannot form itself again around words,
when language we once knew but now hear as garbled

is broken in parts, broken in parts, language fractured & fissured,

                                                    broken in parts

II.

what to do then, when men and women cannot speak,
when meaning is sawed off clean & language becomes a chimney chute
through which sound sweeps as ash coating everything with a sooty pallor,
before syllables can form in the cave of the spirit that issues words, cadences,
that used to roll out like musical notes off the sweetness tongues suddenly cut
clean to blooming silence, dumb screams there now, oozing blood,
where the silver steel flashed red underneath halloween street lamps,
flies swarming around a gaggle of slit throats

& in the middle of it all a chewed up black pencil of a man,
who stands holding his tongue between his hands,
                        silence surrounding him like a mourning shawl,

& what is the belief holding up his laddering backbone there,

the tongue in his hands now was once a saxophone when whole,
was a blur of fingers whooshing through golden keys of his voice belling
like charlie parker burning riffs quick as michael johnson cruising
solo, lickety-split, his turbo-driven voice used to turn flips,
somersaults, turn around in midair like great olympic figure skaters,
their bodies doing twists, the moment there alive, fused
with magic, probed limits of the tongue, unpredictable as mystery,
it once moved to re-create itself, again & again, through improvisation,
sought to push the edge of its creation out beyond boundaries of what
anything would allow, the vocabulary flowing back & forth,
like a mantra, before silence cut through
its song, turned it into ripples on the surface of a river, gone
after a rock dropped through its shimmering, wet skin, through a vortex,
where the eye now catches a language of shadows, once lengthening,
now they are breaking apart in waves of fragmentation

III.

but we can speak with our eyes, can fashion them into a tongue,
can turn that tongue into a living voice that conjures up song,
conjures up spirits, the drumbeat of strong hearts goosing everything along,
like a great drummer keeping time, evenly kept, pulsating breath, strong,
sluicing through the tempo of the lungs,
through death we can travel backward to ancestors through our spirits,
through our mind's juju, we can go down to the station of resurrection,
wait for the underground train marked with vèvès to arrive there,
we can board that train, dream ourselves into magic through imagination,
can walk inside history longside power sleeping deep down inside us, now,
deeper still, deeper than the limits of fear ever allowed us to travel,
because our black cat's bone knows the mojo spirit is listening,
knows the mojo bone can rest in our hands if we dream ourselves deeper,
deep enough to dream ourselves into beauty, deeper still, go down deeper,
deeper, so we can conjure up the power of that black mojo hand,
deeper, so we can restore speech to a severed tongue cut off in a storm
by buzz saw slivers of glass propelled through the dark,

by the awesome power of a tornado's wind,
or cut off by evil, unhuman men, who think love is a gun, a bloody knife
salvation, we can conjure up the power of a black mojo hand, can reconnect
flesh with flesh, expression, can beat human madness with our own magic,
voodoo, can reconnect these islands of words floating through broken
sentences, fractured & fissured, broken apart,
words floating like drowned faces bloated after a sudden flood brought death,
we can reconnect these words & fashion a language out of silence, space,
a language of fragments that can float in the air like chords,
echoing the music of monk's genius, miles, we can hear it if we listen,
can feel it if we listen, can reconnect that pencil-thin black man's tongue,
once a saxophone's voice, can stitch that voice back together again into song,
into music again with a needle stitching love, can weave magic
fashioned there out the bone of a mojo-hand,
can put it all back together again if we listen & feel love,
sluicing poetry & voodoo out of a mojo hand singing through a tongue rooted
                                        within the spirit of healing,
magic & mystery, the song becoming beauty, so listen to beauty
beating in your own human hearts, listen to the healing
powers fashioned from bone of our own mojo hand

    IV.
& the music is jabber-walking across space & air
& comes whispering
& whispering comes carrying
the burden of silence with it for so very long,
beyond this whispering of echoes,
is a wish to reconnect this language, this tongue broken in parts,
broken articulation, beliefs, clues, broken into islands of words,
phrases, isolated beyond meaning, now
silence breaking into sound that is guttural, blues seeded,
inside timbre of the voice rising now to form some kind of language,
it is reaching for beauty, trying to unify fragments
into complete sentences,
though broken apart it is trying to coalesce,
come back together again, for love,

for beauty, for family, so listen
for words that float up from the abyss into recognizable sound that evokes
familiar faces, that are pulled out of a raging, flooded river,
see recognition now in those blinking eyes,
magic unfolding in language rising up there, now guttural but pure,
is reborn here as the tongue is restored, reconnected,
speech returned to voice
inside the mouth,
& now words form that roll off the tongue,
carry faces carved from history,
faces that string themselves together to fashion a memory,
a memory that is a necklace of love beads draped around our necks,
imagine those faces as metaphors now, seeds
for love songs whispering,
tonguing now just outside your ear,
imagine those words as possible healing powers,
a healing love song, whispering now,
whispering, inside your ear

        v.
language is rolling off the tongue now.
acril le la, cra cra, acril le la, ah booka sonday, listen,
the song sings, the bird/man sings way up above the blue,
above the blues, but rooted in those funky dues,
miles playing the blues while the wind is sleeping deep down inside
his blue trumpet, voice, the sound haunting
deep down inside the blues, ah booka sonday,

the wind grows deeper in thunder,
the day puts on its clothing of golden laughter,
wearing its golden flames up there in the blue, travels around spring-
time sewing bright green manes, everywhere, sewing sweet magic back
into the breath, stitched through a voice of blue mystery, is your tongue,
your cockadoodle do, soukas turning flips inside your ears,
is your gin & tonic blues, universal diva,

wearing a deep blue dress any day, a flower in her hair
like lady day singing "strange fruit,"
these are the songs forming in the throat

these are the songs, ah booka sonday

    VI.
& these songs are you turned inside out,
your tongue reconnected now, your voice yourself,
echoing you resurrected, your words carrying faces
you pulled from the river of memory,
from the blood of your own healing your language comes

                                          fusing longing & love

& kisses the day now dressed in blue & green & light,
kisses the day now dressed in who-do-you-love, flight,
the bird/man singing through you

from way up above the blues, above the light,
the distance traveled from him to you now, a clue unlocking
golden traces of solos, pulsating light,

& miles is a moonshot covering the musical distance

from your own heartbeat to this solo, speaking here,
your own language zipping through as pure sound, zigzagging
lightning bolts zipping up the night, is your own solo here riffing,
acril le la, cra cra, acril le la,

sound, beat, thumping through your own voice,
creating inside the drumbeat of your own heart,

& it is you singing now, as a poet,

is your own reconnected tongue, singing

FESTIVAL DAY AT LAGUNA PUEBLO

for George Lewis & the Dancers at Laguna Pueblo

I.

we leave san dia's mountain ranges behind back-dropping
albuquerque like a large spread-out spanish accordion hand-fan,
leave piled into three cars that move like bats out of hell
speeding through wide-open new mexico country,
we pass foreheads of red sandstone, eyes climbing up them to mesas,
before dropping back down & sweeping back out over scorched desert,
to see by the side of the road lizards licking out tongues for insects,
see here & there smashed carcasses of something run over time
& time again, under grinding wheels of bulleting steel environments,
piloted by nervous drivers who probably thought they hit *sleeping policemen*
posing as speed bumps in the road, before they were made flat as bad food,
came to resemble this *smashed something* here,
resting on tar, the winding road in front of us snaking
between hills, whose faces are landslides of crumbling rocks,
fronted by scrub bush, cacti, & wire-link fences
strung out over the land like musical staffs crisscrossing
telephone poles, that resemble christian crosses strung together,
with buzzing wires carrying conversations along interstate forty,
where we travel now fast as speeding bullets ripping through
brains, shot clear through light west toward laguna pueblo,
we pass rio puerto, where a little white cloud hovers over a mesa,
like a spaceship would
in one of those hollywood flying saucer b movies,
just before the ladder eased down
        & deposited all those weird little bulb-headed, big-eyed people
                up in all that blue, a half-moon winking down, half-hidden,
all magical up in all that early morning blue haze
& bright glaring heat,
while off to the side a fifty-car chain-link train eases by, crosses our vision
like a bunch of cockroaches strung together across a kitchen floor at night,
as the wind suddenly kicks up dirt devils out in the desert,

slingshots tiny pelting rocks & sand at our caravan
flying west, lickety-split toward laguna pueblo,
toward whatever we think we might find for ourselves
out here—maybe our true memory?—located somewhere
amongst all these indian legends, scorched mute rocks
(the wind's tongue licking off names of geronimo, crazy horse,
cochise, & sitting bull, their ghosts sitting crosslegged somewhere up,
            perhaps high on some hidden mesa, talking to eagles, circling
hawks, under a cloudless sky, on a crystal blue day,
dreaming of buffalo spirits, long gone like their land, as spent arrowheads
    in the sand point in the direction of where the holy dances used to take place,
where tips of feathered lances jabbed up into
all that remarkable blue covered with white men's blood,
stood straight & tall, held up by warriors whooping war cries, victory calls,
all that gone now, only voices of shivering ghosts remain here mimicking
announcements of fall's fickle winds, just before they turn
cold & scream down white from alaska in winter—)

hawks & eagles circling silently above the walking mute-faced,
still proud indians, who are making their way to the scorched white square
in laguna pueblo (which we are flying toward now
like bats out of hell), carrying memories of the old powerful medicine,
dances that used to conjure up magic imagination wherever their feet shuffled
& hopped, propelled their bodies up into the air to float
& dig down deep into the old power of their memory & history
& fly like magical birds soaring & gliding through their dreams,
as they do now, here, in this sacred place called laguna pueblo,
the place we are flying like bats out of hell to get to, now

II.

& we might have thought it was the highway that brought us here
but in the end it was history, our curious imaginations dragging
our bodies along for the ride, to arrive here at the laguna pueblo festival,
        to watch ferris wheels turn & spin like tops,
as people from all over the indian nation—
navaho, zuni, acoma, & laguna—moved in & out & between
anglos, blacks, & chicanos come to eat greasy fry bread, green & red chili peppers,
all under a broad blue, windswept sky, come to see
dancers gathered in a square behind cracked, slouching huts bleached
white by the sun's maiming, dragon tongue licking down fire,
a fire that reminds indians of the religion spaniards taught them,
in this old, leaning adobe church
(& where the dancers are gathered outside of now),
when they brought them new gods of catholicism from the old world,
brought them to their knees with skewed bibles, disease, & muskets,
turned their once fierce eyes inside out to sadness, to sell their war lances
without tips once covered with white men's blood, sell them, now,
as souvenirs—keepsakes, to cover white men's suburban walls, along-
side bows & arrows, hawk- & eagle-feathered war bonnets, too-
old secrets locked in looks of cosmic pain mute behind impenetrable
looks on faces, that mask all matter of things once thought to be miracles,
all for sale here & now, at the laguna pueblo festival,
where indians wait for power, magic of their dreamers & dancers,
where indians wait for the white man's dreams to turn to ashes,
turn to ashes, on a day, legend has it, that is coming, legend has it,
& is coming very soon & the dancers & medicine men will announce it,
will tell the people today when that day is near, my friend,
& legend has it it is coming very soon, they all say,
legend has it it is coming & very soon

III.

& in an instant we hear the call of five drummers summoning
the dancers,
        & the lead caller lays down rhythms of a chant,
it is in time with bells & olive shells clanging & shaking,

the hawk dance begins to move
        with buffalo & eagle dancers keeping spirits alive,
animal & bird spirits, trilling calls, mysterious as way back then,
when breath left their bodies so long ago, as in song

turquoise blue & bright red colors swim in beige & black,
feathers licked up teased by a breeze spread out before us now,
as male eagle dancers fan their wings in formation,
as buffalo male dancers wave their bows with no arrows,
as fox female dancers wave their arrows with no bows,
as a male fox dancer wearing the head of a fox as a headdress steals by
waving his staff of eagle claws appointed to him as the lead dancer,
his voice chants a call, which is the rhythm shuffling feet move to now,
which is the call buffalo dancers used to dance to way back then,
which they dance too, here, right now—
which is the call—& they are holding
bows & arrows above their heads,
towing spirits attached to their bodies, they float up, come down
as their feet kick up dirt from the scorched earth,
& they are rising once again, floating, their arms are outspread as wings,
their feet shuffling in a circle as hawks & eagles do in the sky,
they are answering the call of ancestor-spirits,
they are answering the call of buffalo-eagles,
they are answering the call of hawks circling high up above,
their heads up in the room of blue sky & they are circling
now, deep in their memory, they are what they remember
& imagine themselves to be, here & now, they are ancestor-spirits
come forth from the other world,
are buffalo & eagle spirits, hawk & wolf & fox & whatever
they imagine themselves to be right now, come forth from power of magic,
are the meaning of feathers, are the symbols of beauty, power, & magic,
come back, are the meaning of red as sun & black representing clouds
& blue the sky & white mother earth
& now they are eagles & hawks circling, here & now,
they have left their bodies on the ground
& are circling as hawks & eagles, here & now,
they are circling, have come back here,

& here & now, they are circling like hawks up in the blue,
they are circling, their arms outspread, their feet shuffling,
they have come back down now & are fox & wolf
baying at the moon, right here, right now,
in dragon-tongued sunlight, they are buffalos
making one last spirit run, they are buffalos
making one last spirit run, here & now
& they are circling, they are circling

IV.
& now the dances are over, the spirits gone back to where-
ever they came from, the hawks & eagles circling high up above
& we are leaving laguna pueblo, we are leaving,
we are leaving the sacred dancers, here & now,
we are leaving,
we are leaving them here but carrying their memories
with us, we are leaving,
        we are leaving the sacred ground,
we are leaving,
we are leaving the call of drummers,
                     we are leaving the spirits behind,
but taking them with us, we are leaving,
we are leaving the spirit of hawk & eagle, we are leaving,
we are leaving the spirit of wolf & fox, we are leaving,
but we are carrying their spirits with us,
leaving, we are carrying the magic
of their mystery with us,
we are leaving,
we are leaving the holy ground,
we are leaving,
we are leaving the spirit dance of ancestors,
                    we are leaving,
we are leaving the holy ground,
we are leaving,
        we are leaving, carrying whatever we can with us,
we are leaving,
we are leaving the holy ground, we are leaving,

we are leaving the holy ground,
we are leaving

        v.

we are leaving the consecrated scorched grounds, we are moving,
moving past hornos adobe ovens brought over by spaniards,
which were passed on to them by arabs
                                    & we are moving
                    past booths of clothes, jewelry, food, & colors overloading

our senses glued to great food smells blooming out here now
from an old navajo lady's stove, whose house we have stopped at
to visit, an old strong painting of sitting bull
                        dominating the white wall of her living room,
while four mexican chihuahua dogs barking up a storm scamper around
the room furiously, busy as mocking-
birds beating their flimsy wings in a constant blur
outside her window, as rock-hard sandstone hills loom up as background,
a blue sky unfurling itself overhead like an endless flag, red, white, & black
clothes flap frenzy on a straight clothesline, taut as a whiplash
strung above deer tracks, outside the old lady's window—
& the deer tracks remind me of old hieroglyphics from egypt—
a hawk circles its airplane shadow above the hard land full of potholes,
recall a scarred ruined face of a man serving three life sentences for murdering
with no remorse, no tête-à-tête, siamoise, vis-à-vis here, nobody pushing
the envelope for amnesty out here, but a brutal life
made even more sinister as the crow flies south
& the snows return as "the hawk's" beaked breath bites down hard
& cold as a well digger's naked asshole exposed in february,
when the wind is a litany of shivering voices, trembling chants
sluicing through laguna, moving through winter

& we've left the dancing behind, & we are moving,
moving to the tune of "hit the road jack,"
on our way back to albuquerque, as the crow flies east,
we are moving down interstate forty, pass signs announcing
paseo del vulcan, tucumcari, santa rosa,

moving east as the crow flies pass parijito, canoncito reservation,
leaving behind the old lady's food that made us drool like fools—
george driving east fast as a baseball thrown by satchel paige
moving toward sandia mountains,
shaped now, from here like watermelons—
we are moving across the rio grande river, pushing on into albuquerque

we have left the magic behind
                            in laguna pueblo,

have left the sacred dancers there, too,
        have left them on their hallowed ground
but we are carrying their memories with us,
are carrying the call of their drummers,
                            are carrying their spirit of hawk & eagle,
we are carrying
their spirits of fox & buffalo, wolf, hawk, & eagle,
        we are carrying the magic of their memory & mystery
with us, we are carrying the spirit dance of their ancestors
with us, we are carrying their poetry from holy ground,
we have left the laguna pueblo & we are singing,
we have left carrying their spirits with us & they are singing,
we have left carrying magic with us & it is singing

we have left the sacred, mysterious ground
& we are carrying the memory of their beauty with us
& it is singing

inside this poem, & it is singing,

singing inside this poem

& it is singing

    —fall 1996

POEM FOR A VOICE ALWAYS IN PRAYER
for Salif Keita

imagine a high-pitched clear voice shouting in the middle
of a malian plain, around the village of djoliba,
a plain dotted with fruit trees, fine grains of hot sand,
pebbles of white quartz, imagine that voice alone there shouting
to beat the band, in the middle of scorched summer days, see a white-
black ghost of a child shouting monkeys away from banana & fruit trees,
people thinking him crazy until all the monkeys leave lickety-split dropping pee,
this black-white african boy who would have been sacrificed because of fear,
if not for his royal bloodline stretching back like the niger river,
because of the big power of collective fear, of being an african ghost child who
shouted monkeys down out of banana, fruit trees, because the people were afraid,
this eerie ghost boy with the royal bloodline going back to soundiata keita,
founder of the mandinka people, now imagine that boy as a shouting
spirit, whose ghost face floated through the darkness like his voice
to mingle with ancestral ghosts up in baobab trees,
balafons strings trembling lyrical as leaves
up in trees stirred by ghost voices & breezes, now imagine
                              an african ghost boy, whose face floats
through the darkness like his voice, who tried to touch God
with his voice, who shouted monkeys out of trees,

in a village that is afraid of his strange power, his difference,
a child who always tried to coexist with God,
in harmony, the voice growing more plaintive, clear, pure as it grew,
as the years blew by like sahilian harmattans in the north of mali, the voice
grew translucent as a scrim, through which an ancestral memory now flowed
whole & beckoned, powerful as the history of heat, the shouts
those monkeys heard, the voice now dreaming of water, surging as currents
of a wide, powerful river around mopti, where the voice now lived,
as a husband & a father & a griot with a guitar
after bamako & the rail band & paris, near a river that has carried histories
up & down its wet back under boats, from timbuktu down to mopti, the niger-
bani flowing wide there as dreams of cool drinks of water

up in the desert north, where the dragon-tongue heat is regular & fierce,
now imagine that voice again as salif keita's voice, a voice always in prayer now,
a voice that passes through your senses & goes straight to the heart,
as that shout once went straight to the hearts of monkeys,
it now enters the spirit as a gift, as a breath of cleansing air, light,
as a song shaped by rolling syllables that ring transcendent
as bells, lyrical as koras & balafons, it is swelling,
it is golden, it wraps itself around your spirit
as would a shower raining down vowels and consonants,

the voice as its own instrument, as the lope of an antelope is magic
the voice dances through air as prayer, as spirit riding the wind as mystery,
the gong of the voice inside rope-a-dope language, inside song,
like a po-inchworm hitching a ride, burrowing along from dusk
to dawn, it is now galloping inside a zebra, the voice there almost religious,
is religious & is talking to you now in prayer,
jambalaya fandango soliloquies from mali, is a gong voice singing,
riffing through malian air by the juju man keita, whose ghost face floats through
the darkness like a song, hear a voice there with wings beating up inside winds,
beautiful as prayer, the spirit dancing down roads,
is alone now with secrets of magic, mystery, is a shaman man
shouting to beat the band, singing from his knees now, his white-black
ghost face floating through the darkness like his song, is high-pitched,
powerful as the history of heat, we must pass through the song,
its mystery & its magic & its heat, is the history of us all now

& it sings jambalaya fandango prayers, the juju ghost man from mali,
his cadence & language the rope-a-dope lope of an antelope,
in the air it shouts soliloquies once heard by monkeys, is a voice always in prayer,
powerful & pure as harmattan sand storms, it always goes straight to the heart,
is a winged voice free as syllables of the wind

& is always going straight to the heart,

imagine salif keita, a white-black ghost man whose face floats through
the darkness like his song, his voice always arrowing straight to the heart,

his winged voice always a song, always a prayer, imagine salif
keita, imagine a winged voice, golden & always in prayer

& always arrowing with total belief toward the heart

is always arrowing with total belief, to enter the heart

BELLS
   after Gustaf Sobin

eye am hearing bells in the music of poetry, bells
inside laughter tinkling like silver, bells rinsed in colors, shapes
& forms washing wave after sonorous wave, bells washed through
wind chimes, swept through morning's first breaking light, rolling
bells shivering in damp cool speech hip language seduces
& imitates, bells coursing through syllables spilling from lips,
bells tinkling through raindrops, pooling on rooftops,
spreading like rosebuds, airborne on wind tongues,
drooling down storm drains, riding water through whirlpools,
drop by dropping drop, bells spooling electric
through hearts in sacred himalayan mountains of tibetan buddhists, bells
swirling through pooling deep eyes of lovers, trilling inside bright voices
raised by small children, bells seducing through winds that play games
with our minds, with the way we hear time slipping through our ears,
& there are bells heard in kisses when sucking lips meet, vibrating,
electric bells, silver bells, breeze-blown bells that tongue
through fragrant afternoons of spring/time,
bells in silver dewdrops shimmying down bright green leaves
that land & float like rafts skimming surfaces of glass-blue rivers,
bells that dive through sparkling waterfalls like voices or solos
rinsed with clear welling sounds that tickle our senses
like crystal runs of bill evans laying down clues, bells sluicing through,
in flight, the way a thief steals through the night's deep music like a sleuth,
the way blues tiptoes over piano keys dropping bell notes here
& there as chords shimmy-shangling through the thick night air rinsed
in shimmering, electric beauty, bells that render us spellbound,
as when the heart seduces sound by locking up pure
rhythm that is light, conjuring bells that speak in voices dazzling,

church bells that ring inside seductive sweet strides of dancing women,
as when bells roll through their hips swaying lyrical, incredible magic, & eye
heard bells in heat of summer language making sweet flowers rise,
heard bells in the voice of pavarotti's "nessun dorma,"
heard bells clanging & rolling through the square fronting westminster abbey,
heard bells in the sound of african dew mornings rising, trumpets blaring,
heard bells in the silver ice of hale-bopp's streaking comet tail,
heard bells ringing throughout plazas of freedom everywhere—
but not from the cracked fluke bell squatting mute in philadelphia—
heard bells inside all beauty heard or seen anywhere,
bells, bells, splendid sweet bells,
heard bells in the seduction of great poetry singing,
heard bells ringing through the luminous language of sweet birds
riffing, bells, bells, splendid sweet bells,
swelling inside the air's sweet music

V

CHORUSES

for Allen Ginsberg, 1926 – 1997, and Lucy Goldman

I.

within the muted flight of daybreak, inside its leaked, trembling light
of birth, after the cracked shell of night's dome has split open,
cut loose a flurry of pitched voices grown from different, linguistic sperm,
we hear a cacophony of opposing rhythms integrated inside the body of a song,
carried as if upon the widespread feathered wings of a bird across the sky
of imagination, as in the circling, beating mantra the heart knows
as breath becoming choruses, becoming soundtracks
lifted off a poet's chanting tongue, syllables become moments
within moments, are transformed into song
that sings beautiful as any morning glory colors when the sun slants down,
cuts through whatever is there with its golden blades, becomes beams
bright & sharp as voices heard anywhere hands meet drumheads of skin
tightly pulled, the rhythms vibrating there in skimming waves
washing in or out at you as if they were imitating foaming sound rolling in from
the sea, curling tips of its waves into shape of grigri lips that can be cataclysmic
as foam sudsing off lips of madmen moaning, or roaring,
or doing whatever it is that madmen do, in katmandu, in the center
of nepal, or on the streets of new york city, where voices fire up pitches
fast as old satchel paige threw a baseball down the heart of the plate
or snaked it across inside or outside corners disguised as an aspirin,
like sound nicks away edges of language, chips off syllables & meaning,
until the voice cracks words electric as static,
perhaps resembles the sound lightning bolts make when ripping off small pieces
    of dark space & sky
when thunder cracks its jagged whip across the night's high gloom

there, where wolves sing love songs to the moon, where lookeloos crane
their necks on freeways trying to spot hale-bopp comet's streaking silver ice tail,
who listen to songs of beck over the radio hightailing it lickety-split through
this dark out west, burning rubber signatures into asphalt, as cars
wheel in & out of traffic, screech brakes, shape a kind of music, a new language
only the initiate know & imitate as it twists itself around again & again,
doubles-back in the way rhythm turns in & back on itself,

like a concrete pretzel claiming its own place as it curls into space,
lifts off in the shape of interwoven, interlocking freeway ribbons carrying cars
& speech above our heads on conveyer belts as motors screaming high speed
octane, zooming around curves like crazed vagabonds
hitting moments of sweet need, as music fills the air with magical incantations
wrapped in voices that track down sound, then double back blue as terror
recycles itself through years when good old boys guzzled beers
on back roads of america in a slew of cars that sped down roads twisted as limbs
of people suffering from rheumatoid arthritis, gunracks over their faces,
grinning like cheshire cats who just ate a slew of canary birds,
yellow feathers scattered all over that sordid history
& everywhere blood on whiskers of hyenas, blood frozen in ice-
cold stares of serial killers, blood in drawing rooms of politicians practicing
blood sports, bullshitting us in washington, blood on the cheese face of a leering
moon after eclipse hung down over rancho santa fe, blood on grimacing faces
bursting from bloated black bodies in rwanda, blood exploding from that
incinerated house in waco, texas, blood shooting from the eyes of a child before
he pulled the trigger in paducah, kentucky, blood in the speeches of ministers
pontificating from pulpits, blood all up in the curdling screams sliced clean
through by razors, blood smeared all over the blues
choruses of screams heard chilling after explosions in jerusalem,
in the choruses of hand grenades tattooing the nights of bulgaria, colombia,
in the choruses of machine gun bursts stitching the evenings of mexico city,
los angeles, that snuffed out the life of notorious b.i.g., tupac in las vegas,
choruses of fire meeting choruses of bullets, choruses of hand grenades
greeting the imploding language of love, blood on the syllables, choruses
spewing blood on musical notes that sing of these times everywhere

& blood on money pulled from ocean bottoms by deep-sea divers,
blood up in the voices of poets impregnating stanzas with music,
blood on tongues cut off because they sang beautiful images of love,
blood where the land mines littered the earth with eyeballs,
skulls, & severed hands that point accusatory fingers stiff as bones in the mud,
& choruses & blood & choruses & blood, choruses & blood,

behold the time-clocks ticking inside blood irrigating flesh,

inside the moment when the poet knows language as a wellspring,
inside the moment when truth is understood as a two-headed sword that is
duplicitous as the notion there is a true beauty in flesh, lyrical with movement,
final as death, time marches on, leaves' flesh imprinted with maps of spiderweb
sites, that spread across the body's internet, as songs pealing across
this embezzled air tantalize us with history of our continued failure

II.

when we sing we hear & know the music best, hear it with hearts
imitating breath, the rhythm of drumbeats in cadences
true poets hear, the heartbeat of their breath in time signatures spread,
scored like music across fleet pages scrolling the mind, dreams composed within
language, when words become musical notes or chords, language is traced back
where it first burst from song as anchored root,
grew into a melody (a sweet flower smelled in springtime,
summer, when birds clear their throats of seeds, open piccolo beaks
& run tremolos beautiful, at dizzy gillespie speed)

& there is joy in the sweet singing of melodies,
beauty in the voice marveling at the sweet, blessed curves of a lover's
ripe body, in the way a woman's mind is shaped, her thighs, breasts, her lips
caressing in the way a dress might caress the sensuousness of her body,
pure joy in the rapture of her kiss, blood boiling over there with sweet heat,
glory in her song, glory in the choruses of blood singing
beneath her flesh, choruses of heartbeats drumming faster & faster still,
glory in the mind running over from a space rooted in love,
where a poet creates from inside a moment of stillness, silence,
when metaphor is ejaculated from mystery into language,
sluices from the brain as words scaffolded onto the page like archipelagos
strung out in a sea of air like notes blown complete from a bell of a trumpet,
becomes poetry when form connects structure with magic, when breath
carries poetry with the indelible smell of damp rooms after lovemaking,
rumpled sheets stained with semen, history, the claustrophobic odor of cigarettes
when jamming their crooked, burnt-out butts into overflowing ashtrays,
into rooms drenched with stale smell of whiskey & garbage
& all this forms a question mark, a gesture—

a hand curved in space & bent at the wrist—a fragrance of mystery evoking
the color of pastel drenched with lilting speech of the caribbean hinting of soft
seas, the air there filled, fragrant with garlic, peanut oil, saffron,
orange-gold sunsets laced with magenta, pink streaked with magical coral
reefs, purple threaded like veins through blue, the feel of it is a chorus,
is a song lifted from the blood of the sky by a poet who sings
another prayer at sunset, practices ancient science of cabala,
cabala lore, cabala, cabala lore, cabala

III.

& eye heard you passed away today allen ginsberg, heard it over the radio—
like eye heard about miles' passing over the idiot tube—that you went home
surrounded by friends & peace, heard you wrote till you slipped into a coma
after you wrote a last poem called "fame and death,"
you left us great poems allen, poems that fused blues & jewish chants, rock 'n' roll
& jazz riffs you left behind as gifts to remind us of a life lived fast to the fullest,
in "absolute defiance," you were a bridge between the sacred,
the transcendental, the underground demon & the buddhist-shaman-priest,
you were the guru speaking of wars when skulls were used to cradle silver coins
flashing under the light of human skin stretched tight into lampshades
used to filter heat from glaring lightbulbs—& the silver flashing there
like glittering smiles, evil as death—o great bard breathing in & out,
spoken blues chants coursing through your lines gone home to rest,
gone home to rest beside your mother & father in spirit & shivah,
it was a great love you gave us, allen, a great love that makes me remember
you now with affection & awe, o great son of whitman, blake, & williams,
your love of mystery, gemara, your love of flesh & magic, blood of poetry
coursing through choruses of your river-veins, love
coursing through memory of chicken soup, roasted eggs, love,
the smell of challah bread evoking candles burning on the sabbath,
on the lower east side where you walked hip-di-dip, a little strut & bounce
in the dip of your stride, you walked amongst jews wearing yarmulkes—
& though you moved a little odd down there on passover,
buddhist that you were, you still moved,
many of them will still sit seven days of shivah for you,
many will lift their voices in solemn kaddish prayers—

& so eye baptize you here with rhythms of black church gospel,
with rhythms pulled from some of your favorite voices—
ray charles, bessie smith, ma rainey, charlie parker, & john coltrane—
have washed your memory down with holy cadences—cool & hot
as water—rinsed in blues & jazz riffs, chanted from voices
& baptized in holy rivers of cabala, cabala lore,

cabala, cabala lore, cabala, cabala lore

& blood & choruses, blood & choruses,
baptized in rivers of blood & choruses

cabala, cabala lore, cabala, cabala lore

coursing through poetry that burst from your river-veins,
coursing through poetry that burst from your river-veins,

shalom o great mystic bard, shalom

you begin with a sound wrapped around a syllable, or syllables,
a word (or words) like razzmatazz, or ratamacue, then you listen to
a red-boned black man playing a horn like a clue,
like a train or john coltrane or bird, then you play around with sounds
your ears done heard, lift them off a rebound, spellbound inside a rue,
because of a cue your memory remembered & knew,
                                    now you add a few nouns & vowels,
words that sing like birds, who flew through a spring wind thunder clapping,
        with roiling, rolling consonants, their feathers echoing colors now
black or white or blue, as a ranky dank pressing flesh beneath them
was immune to trailing blues stretched out behind him,
voices that flew rhythmic as queued soundtracks through the night's
sweet longing, choo-chewing like wailing engines hurtling down isolated
                tracks, way out in the dead of night's hushed music,
            around the voodoo, bewitching hour of bats, who like words
bruising from a crew of mad hatter good old boys were circling inside
a hushed cave, where a strange blend of language was fashioning itself now
from cries & screams, the whooshing of beating wings
& white robes drumming pell-mell clues through
        the dark cinematography of a dream bordering on nightmare,
as it wraps itself around you now as would a cocoon,

you find yourself there inside the cave of your head
& you are whatever it is you think you are there, brand new,
you are what you believe in as truth, right then, right there,
when you hear sheets of sound rushing out of the bell of a saxophone,
it is a stomp down cornucopia of magic spiraling out of a dream,
from a golden axe, shaped like an elephant's trunk, the shape of need here
is a question mark bewitching us with breath, power, mystery, stealth,
is what new language is shaping itself into now inside the neon air
hip-hopping & rapping in voice rhymes of young people,

before us right now is what the mind's ear reminds the tongue of here,
chasing the sound of a freight train moving at full speed, is a syntax,
a jackety-jack of wheels rolling through the slick flow of tracks bedazzling gears,
the song of it all beguiling us with amazement, the rackety-rack of steel spinning
over & down rails, underground or overground, tracks,
                                        the sound we hear is real when we know it
coming from the terrifying mystery of a hip shaman's horn,
we see the music form in the shape of the hot tongue of a bic flame lighter
tonguing out gushed heat,
            flames as sounds, as words inside the scorched flow of lava,
inside a tongue that is red, white, & blue, laced with dues paid in philadelphia,
    in hamlet, north carolina, where a language was fractured there,
congealed, until it hopscotched itself to its own back beat
conundrum, before it pealed across the air clear as a bell ringing cold
on sundays, unleashed a rage in rhythm & tempo, heated voices in sermons,
became a fire there in flight, was volcanic with syllables aglow, the night
flaming with embers washing through the breeze like a tribe of fireflies
swarming the night sky, a voice pure & guttural,
            a primal scream looping clues of prophecy here, blue,
or sweetly singing as a slew of birds
                tracking across a fondued sky laced with magenta,
their music heard in ringing silver bells as the wind tongue trills melodic
as it breezes lilting language through chiming leaves that tremble

like lovers in heat/time, when the air is all aglow & splendiferous
with greens, yellows, & golds,
                bright reds of bougainvilleas,
jacarandas fragrant as voices of doves cooing, sweet pink of flaring
rhododendrons that burst into shapes of trumpet bells evoking
miles playing muted live in memory, clean as a whistle,
is where a poet stretches rubber sentences into bridges of music now,
language reinventing itself daily out of lost & found words,
constructing what it is to speak as a true american here,

today, right now, words moving through poems as magicians through parades,
clowns dressed up as verbs, adverbs, adjectives surrounding nouns with bright
verve, reminds the senses of sweet odor of frangipani perfume,
rhymes & rhythms intoxicating the senses,

this moment sluicing across the air in a rainbow of races,
seductive with music, images moving quickly as faces in an mtv video,
across screens blazing fast as beats moved through bebop, urban slick
as hip-hop brothas chilling wicked in blooming fubu color schemes
rad in baggy jeans, their hand jive flicking & stabbing the air, constantly blur-
                    ring images—blink & they're gone like pop goes the weasel—
their rhythms nicking edges off slick time in stop-gap measures,
voices locking & leaking into currency, flip & zip,
can-you-dig-it, inside blaring boxes clocking backbeats stitching threads
through the culture of hip-hop, attitudes holding everything together there,
as when a guitar player picks blaze out of funk noise,
his cadence up inside & outside time,
as in this poem swinging its voice downwind to cross fragile bridges
strung together with cadences & words, structures underneath
form the bass-groove swaying back & forth over deep chasms,
between mountains of language, where a child hears vocabulary in a swing,
in the backyard of a favorite uncle waxing real with his sho-nuff-to-god,
hope-to-die-ace-boon-coon-throw-downs,
                    the ones that always got his back each & every
time he smacks scary, wherever he goes, their attitudes high-fivin their eyes
& everything silent here except the wind's screaming terror,
words trying to cross over to the other side, to where the nephew swings,
                    right here, right now, words flowing through seamless
as eye (w)rap my tongue around a bridge of johnny ace or nat king cole
stitching together a profusion of sweet cadences frank
sinatra & elvis stole, words that breathe inside a living language full of colors,
as choirs of birds singing atop hot telephone wires carry aretha's gospel,
a symphonic elocution of elegant voices,
          a cecil taylor bedazzlement of lyrical, discordant chords,
swinging double-bladed axes cutting down trees as they slice through all this
blue air, the bird man still singing now over steel tracks
snaking through & in between landscapes, where tupac & biggie now sleep

beside coaltrain(s) blowing through the night's voodoo air, sweet
the feeling here now, still blue as you were charlie parker,
& truly american as slow trains choo-chooing twelve bar blues
through your old stomping ground of kansas city's twelfth & vine,
where you first showed your razzle-dazzle,

      your feathers spreading their beauty through wind-chimes,
aching with your soliloquizing voice, always on edge,
triple-timing the fire that flowed through your genius ire on time,
until a chicken bone stuck itself inside your throat & damned up your music,
(like that legendary finger stuck in that dike did to tupac, did to biggie, too)
pure smack snaking venom through your veins,
in a deadly slow dance with death you stumbled & scratched,
poisoned your brain until your head nodded off for real, then the bells tolled,
but boy did you jam, jam, boy did you jam until you left, no sweat, boy did you
jam, jambo, jambalaya, gumbo, boy did you jam jam, boy did you jam
& play that horn for real before the pain jammed vomit in your throat,
left those hot cadences cold as methuselah,
fire bird of stricken-heat, chicken-gumbo boy of sound language, boy,
did you jam, jam, boy did you jam, boy did you jam, jam, boy did you jam
riffs run through scales & chords, inverting electric

everything you heard you turned inside out, structures,
blew past every note—& through them, too—
rooted them in your own blue expression of turn everything inside out,
you jambo, gumbo, chicken-liver boy, running up & down jambalaya scales,
pastiche, a coaltrain before coltrane blew down the hushed voodoo night,
a coaltrain burning across flat plains of kansas city, flight & barbecue
sauce up in the flavor of your drenched hot giddiup, scorching as red pepper
chili sauce, yo boy of bebop phrasing in *groovin' high,* you blew:

bebop, bebop, beedoo beeboli, doodle-li, bebop, bebop,
beedoo beeboli, doodle-li, bebop, bebop,
beedoo beeboli
                    bop baw baw baw bo de baaaaaaaaa daaaaaaa . . . .

& you ran it all the way to new york city, minton's & birdland,
chicken eating boy turned hip man skeedaddleing choochooing chords,
so fast the air could hardly digest them, not to mention some human
ears, playing *salt peanuts, salt peanuts,*
you & diz beautiful beyond words tradin' fours in duet,
fours in traffic, boppin & rappin before tupac & biggie were even born

bird, you uptown in harlem creating language that reinvented itself again
& again before rap seduced rhythms down to scratching old records & words,
skating over samples of james brown & george clinton, toasting & roasting
the language like you & diz did in a *dizzy atmosphere,* jammin'

beedle-loo-beedle-loo-beedle-loo-bop,
beedle-loo-beedle-loo-beedle-loo-bop,
beedle-loo, beedle-loo-beedle-loo-bop,
beedle-loo, beedle-loo
beedle-loo-beedle-loo-beedle-loo-bop,
beedle-loo-beedle-loo-beedle-loo-bop,
beedle-loo-beedle-loo-beedle-loo-bop,
beedle-loo, beedle-loo

words & sounds that built bridges toward a new tongue,
& it all started back in africa, mixed with europe over here, everything else
that found itself here, too, in this gumbo stew, jambalaya,
this salad bowl filled with all kinds of flavors,
this pastiche, collage of language reinventing itself every day,
every moment giving itself props, wherever words are
spoken, patch themselves together with sound, form a sentence,
that becomes a musical line perhaps lifted from armstrong, bird, or miles
a phrase snatched & grafted into language of tupac & biggie, buzzing
in the attitudes of alanis morrisette or jamiroquai scatting
phrases metamorphosed into dance when he reaches back
to grab hold of a language to swing & sing

today, in this moment in time, when everything is evolving,
right now, from cue tips of tongues, a new language
is waiting for you to discover listener, for you to give it some props,
to speak it, wrap your tongue around it, roll it off your assembly line of new
expressions too, so give it up for the new, right here, right now, so speak it,
don't diss it, give the new some props right now,
freak it out with your own
dash of flavor,   .
                          say what's up in the air as sound, now
know that it's rooted & shaped in the vortex of change-truth
which is constant with language & words, sounds & attitude, now
say what's birthing in the womb of air, now
say what's birthing in the womb of air, now:

bustin on the scene clockin banji beastie boys actin like fiends:
down with the fave, funky jam, the noise up in the legit
jack up, someone screaming to kill the ill funky noise living large,
with an ace keepin it real, poppin the rip, doin the nasty to the bump
breakdown in the bricks, where the homies roll bones
to clock dollars, chillin hard through the calendar, gangstas flexin
profiles, while they kick it on the real decked in doo-doo pants
saggin slow like low riders over their doggy-grips
as they watch aces ball with the pill takin it hard to the rack,
skyin down the box, risin up like god to deal, or flash for the count,
pumpin treys from downtown, nothin but nets

words that build bridges toward a new tongue

beedle-loo-grab-a-groove-drop-some-slick-talk,
jazz-a-phrase-pop-a-blues-new-as-hip-hop,
cruisin-through-rapping-clues-sprung-from-bebop
me-&-you, grooving through
me-&-you, groovin through

me-&-you, singin new . . . . .